The History of The Philadelphia Mafia

• •

Before Bruno

●●●●●●●●●●●●●●●●●●●●●●●●●●●

The
History
of
The Philadelphia Mafia

Book One: 1880–1931

●●●●●●●●●●●●●●●●●●●●●●●●●●

CELESTE A. MORELLO

Library of Congress CIP Data: 00-130483

ISBN: 0-9677334-1-3 (Volume 1)

Cover design by CAM and Frank J. Szerbin shows photographs of law enforcement officers and criminals indicted in Philadelphia during Prohibition.
Source: *Public Ledger.*

Printed in the United States of America

Contents

• •

List of Illustrations

●●

Preface
●●●●●●●●●●●●●●●●●●●●●●●●●●●●●●●●●●●

The research done for this work was completed to produce an extensive, comprehensive history of Philadelphia's
Mafia. The work documents years of relationships among
the Families (i.e., units of Mafiosi, and later, La Cosa
Nostra [LCN] members) and among various other groups;
and it recounts what they imparted as memories of an organization that no longer exists. It is a history of what
Prohibition, Benito Mussolini and the modern age have
destroyed. Because there has never been a history written
about Philadelphia's Mafia and LCN, this work attempts to
relate this city's crime Families to their contemporaries in
other Families, whether in the urban or rural areas in the
United States.

Angelo Bruno was the most well-publicized leader of
Philadelphia's Mafia/La Cosa Nostra Families. He represented the city and parts of southern New Jersey in underworld activities from late 1959 until his untimely death on
March 21, 1980, while securing an historical place as
Philadelphia's first boss to provide a public record of some
of his relationships with the news media, law enforcement

and some well-known peers in New York. Capriciously called "The Gentle Don" by the press, Bruno was also referred to as a "Greaser," despite that he was very American in his ways, using his ingenuity with capitalism to found one of the East Coast's most lucrative illegal and legal enterprises. And he laid the groundwork for Philadelphia's Mafia/LCN to operate on a level which no one before or after him has been able to sustain.

But before Bruno there were many bosses, each who contributed to the Sicilian American Mafia and then to the LCN, another course of criminality during their individual tenures. Not every Mafia/LCN boss who ran the Philadelphia Family before Bruno was known, but those who have been identified by law enforcement are described within these pages.

This is essentially a social history of conveyance—of cultural ideals and cultural practices. When immigrants from western Sicily arrived in southeastern Pennsylvania, hardly anyone understood their traditions and language. These Sicilians alone, from the island's western half, brought the Mafia: theirs was a tradition unknown in eastern Sicily and on mainland Italy. With each successive decade of western Sicilians settling here, new adaptations arose in how this foreign culture would be integrated into an American culture that changed faster with each major technical innovation. Two world wars created shifts in life styles, personal outlooks and individual roles in society. But within a subcultural group such as the Sicilian American Mafia, and later with the hybrid La Cosa Nostra, the effects of cultural change would be more significant with the accession of each boss within each Family. Leading these underworld activities in Philadelphia were the representatives or bosses, who laid a foundation for all of the present LCN's sources of power and wealth.

It began with these men who came before Bruno.

Historiography

●●●●●●●●●●●●●●●●●●●●●●●●●●●●●●●●

The Mafia and its U.S. counterpart, La Cosa Nostra (LCN), have aroused scholarly debates in numerous criminological theories as well as in its many presumptuous histories. As late as 1997, former Pennsylvania Crime Commission officials Charles Rogovin and Frederick T. Martens commented on the "shallowness of historical research on organized crime," which included the Mafia and LCN.[1] Sociologist Howard Abadinsky likewise agreed that there is much written on organized crime history, which includes the Sicilian American Mafia and LCN, but "quantity cannot replace quality, and the latter is the major problem."[2] Recognizing this void led none of the aforementioned to contribute constructively to this history.

Aside from the rather confined areas of academic speculation that involved the theoretical frameworks, (most of which have been discredited in recent years[3]), the popular press seemed to remain the most consistent source of some type of an account on the Mafia and LCN because this record has not been subjected to the same purges as criminal records. Periodic culling of local and state law enforcement records has certainly impeded long-range statistics, leaving the press to provide details on certain criminal incidents. Yet, despite the Mafia and LCN's role in popular culture, there is some concern for competence, cohesion and credibility in all forms of data—these elements sometimes were overshadowed by the media's appeal to the emotions in their newspaper accounts. But these records proved at the least, points of reference.

Notwithstanding this, all sources are posed to be criticized. But in the case of Philadelphia's Mafia sources, several high hurdles were presented which would seemingly be insurmountable to researchers. In the city's overall criminal history, some of the primary sources were suspect and led to an unpredictable course of research which required further labor in the process of establishing credibility. The news media, though the only continuous source of information of criminal activity in Philadelphia, had some usual uncertainties. Far more frustrating was the peculiar scarcity of historical information that could be gleaned from the few existing criminal records in the city. For anyone who sought information about Philadelphia's Mafia and LCN, the only "histories" were to be found in the Pennsylvania Crime Commission Reports and in the indirectly accessible findings of federal law enforcement personnel written in the 1960s, but not in contemporary data. For Philadelphia's crime history record, "the ideological preconceptions of law enforcement agencies" alluded to by Alan Block[4] did negatively and unobjectively influence what was written about the Sicilian American Mafia and LCN. Suspicions become allayed however, when one considers that decades of relationships among Philadelphia's underworld, law enforcement officials and politicians determined whether a criminal record would be written at all. A later record however, by special agents from the Justice Department, reflected views of a higher, less corruptible law enforcement of a different time and documented the local bonding between civil servants and underworld figures. But again, inconsistencies with all of the data prevented the historical facts from placement within a more successive pattern to form a "history."

On the surface then, the history of Philadelphia's Mafia and LCN had been subordinated into a discreet position in relation to New York, Chicago, Detroit and even Cleveland where crime historiography is more consistent. Thus, the only information on Philadelphia's Mafia past for decades was fragmented, and if one could describe it as "historical data" from various law enforcement sources and the press. The record was also incidental, if not accidental in revealing a Mafia in southeastern Pennsylvania which apparently was unworthy of note before the ascendancy of Angelo Bruno in 1959. Researchers could notice in the newspapers and in some criminal records the names of many gangsters in generic groups, using the most recent immigrants such as the "Jewish Mob" and various "Italian" gangs. These dated the sentiments of the time and place, but little else. The Lanzetti brothers, gangsters who were neither Black Handers nor Mafiosi, encouraged more news coverage towards themselves almost as much as anyone in the "Jewish Mob" and nourished local biases, thereby affecting the writing of this history. As it was read, then, crime was associated with the current lower-income or impoverished groups or whoever was considered then as "racially inferior." Consequently, documenting the crime history in Philadelphia has been hampered by the lack of objectivity and honesty among the recorders of history.

In recent decades, and on a more academic level, two schools of thought predominate in the scholarly writing of Mafia and LCN history. Occasionally, Philadelphia's Families and underworld groups were mentioned. Oftentimes incongruous in their findings of historical facts, one school of thought treated the Mafia and LCN in the U.S. solely as criminal entities, while the other school placed the organizations within a socio-political framework. Very little revisionist history in general has been written to date. The subject of the Mafia had previously been handled, as historian Denis Mack Smith summed up in 1968, "as a way of living...[with] complicated social and economic causes" rather than as a "society."[5] Since then, there still has been no marriage between law enforcement's historical record or the criminological theories that unfailingly used fragmented, incompetent historical researches.

However, with reference to Philadelphia, there were some works that would confound rather than contribute in substance to local Mafia/LCN history. One such book was Joseph Albini's *The American Mafia: Genesis of a Legend* (1971), which blatantly denied any Mafia/LCN in the U.S. even after extensive FBI wiretappings made from 1961 to 1965 were made public in *U.S. v. DeCavalcante, et al.* In these tapes, Angelo Bruno and a few other Philadelphia Family members figure repeatedly, and thus counter Albini's theories with their dialogues on organization, activities, networkings and customs. A few years later, the histories presented in Humbert S. Nelli's *The Business of Crime* (1976) and Thomas M. Pitkin's *The Black Hand* (1977) were also at variance with Albini's brief history of the Mafia's origins in the U.S. These works provided more facts about the Mafia, Black Hand and Camorra in the U.S., but hardly on Philadelphia. The FBI's reports from the 1960s, while untimely to incidents and individuals who were active in crime in the early twentieth century, nonetheless were excellent leads and provided data on the Mafia and LCN in Philadelphia from many living witnesses.

Some work of this period attempted to craft sociological frameworks from pieces of historical data. One public document, the Pennsylvania Crime Commission Report of

1970 was, perhaps unknowingly, in conflict with the sociological work produced in 1972 by Francis A. J. Ianni. In
A Family Business, Ianni referred to his doctoral work in
the 1950s on the western Sicilians in Montgomery County,
outside of Philadelphia. He called this his "introduction to
organized crime,"[6] but was reluctant to use the word,
"Mafia" or to pursue these suburban Philadelphians' "organized crime" activities on an historical level. In fact, Ianni's
exposé of these suburban Philadelphians neither prompted
law enforcement to make a record nor inspired local historians to continue a more indepth study. On a national scale,
sociologist Donald Cressey's *Theft Of The Nation* (1969)
recalled just one reference to Philadelphia made by Joseph
Valachi to the U.S. Senate in the 1960s. After the second
Pennsylvania Crime Commission Report appeared in 1980,
sociologist Howard Abadinsky wrote *Organized Crime* and
The Mafia in America, both of which contained "histories"
that ignored Philadelphia's record of Mafia activity and
its Family's interactions with the LCN's most powerful
members in New York and New Jersey.

Efforts to piece together a history of Mafia and LCN
development were equally fruitless by other writers. Nelli's
work disappointedly used a few Philadelphia newspaper
accounts on non-Mafia members as his sources on the local
Mafia and underworld.[7] *The City and The Syndicate:
Organized Crime in Philadelphia* (1985), by Gary W. Potter
and Philip Jenkins of Pennsylvania State University,
scarcely moved beyond the Crime Commission Reports' histories with its rather weak information and even weaker
researching skills. Stephen Fox's *Blood and Honor*, published in 1989, mentioned Philadelphia's underworld during Prohibition but completely evaded the subject of the
local Mafia, its origins and evolution.

Any history on Philadelphia's Mafia and LCN focused
on "law and criminality" instead of on the social, economic,

political and cultural influences on the groups' interrelational involvements, because most of the data had previously been derived from law enforcement sources. The U.S. Government's Third Interim Report, Special Committee to Investigate Organized Crime in Interstate Commerce (1951) and the Kefauver Commission's Conclusion of the same year do not mention Philadelphia's Mafia/LCN's existence, despite civilians' claims to the contrary. In these cases, the local politicians and police hampered the Federal authorities' work to establish essential evidence; otherwise, there were just allegations noted by the press. Equally important for the researcher's consideration is the fact that perhaps a unique tradition existed in Philadelphia beyond simple political corruption. There is barely anything to remark on ethnic bias or prejudice arising from the administrative offices towards Sicilian Mafiosi in the nineteenth to early twentieth centuries. Later, the same trend continues—a quality unmatched with any other major urban center of Mafia/LCN activity in the U.S.[8]

• • • • • • • • •

This history utilizes as primary sources the Department of Justice's Federal Bureau of Investigations' files on the individuals in review. These records contain information that other jurisdictions had long discarded or destroyed. Some State and Treasury Departments' data, public records filed by the Courts, municipal or county offices and churches were researched as well. The Philadelphia press (*Inquirer, Bulletin, Public Ledger, Record* and *Daily News*) were steadfast sources with which to compare information as were the out-of-town newspapers which often complemented them.

The published general histories of Philadelphia are not as satisfactory as one would expect. Patrician scholars in the nineteenth and early twentieth centuries tended to patronize the core elite group of old Quakers and Protestants who were the City Fathers and industrialists; they gave little attention to other social, economic or ethnic classes. The only fairly recent work written on Philadelphia history, by historian Russell Weigley, contained information on the local underworld that was unsupported by numerous sources in law enforcement and by the testimonies of many individuals directly involved with such matters. Philadelphia's police history is from one source published in 1887. Records by social welfare and reform groups were neither direct nor suggestive of the ethnic crime within Philadelphia's neighborhoods. Biographies, though not necessarily considered as scholarly works, were also used as primary sources for background as well as for general information. Nick Gentile, a Mafioso in Sicily and in many U.S. venues, gave a broad history of Mafia activities from the early to mid-twentieth century in *Vita di Capomafia* (1963). Joseph Bonanno's *A Man of Honor: An Autobiography* (1983) contained information from this Sicilian American Mafioso/LCN member's life relative to this text on the Castellammarese War and Family activities in general. Bonanno is quick to refute a number of sources, including Joseph Valachi, the first person to defect from the LCN. In Peter Maas' *The Valachi Papers* (1968), there is a controversial record that nonetheless has important Philadelphia names, but little else.

As rarely as Philadelphia appeared in the secondary sources, the information seemed constantly in conflict with each other, whether historical or sociological in form. As frustrating as the historical interpretations sometimes read, the secondary sources however, sustained some data that was useful after corroborating or debunking them with the primary sources or oral histories. These works included Nelli, Pitkin, Potter and Jenkins, and Fox.

Lastly, this history on the Mafia and LCN should serve to encourage researchers to reconsider the existing literature on the U.S. Mafia and LCN in order to broaden one's thoughts on why this body of work was initially written and for what purpose. The reader will notice that I hesitate to challenge histories written by non-scholars, such as journalists and the like. Presumably, their liability for error is expected to be greater then those in academia in whom we place greater trust.

• • • • • • • • •

Methodology
●●●●●●●●●●●●●●●●●●●●●●●●●●●●●●●●●●●●●●●

Because this work combines the dual schools of thought in treating the Sicilian American Mafia as an historical subject, as well as a social entity, the methodology is appropriately disclosed for discussion.

Donald Cressey once wrote on the challenges faced by social scientists who dared to research organized crime. He bemoaned the "secrecy of the participants, the confidentiality of materials...and the filters or screens on the perceptive apparatus of informants and investigators"[9] which would possibly impede the search for facts. In researching this history, however, I had little reluctance in obtaining information from live witnesses. Because of my ancestry, which I had in common with most of the interviewees, and because of the fact that many of my relatives' lives crossed with theirs, I felt no such restraint in questioning. I conducted oral histories and interviews with several Mafiosi, some of whom made the transition into the LCN; associates of the LCN; relatives and friends of the men in review; law enforcement and government officials; legal professionals; relatives and friends of western Sicilian ancestry; and ordinary individuals who were living during the course of the times in question.

This methodology was not used solely to present a history of how the Mafia and LCN was regarded in literature or by a contemporary public at different times in the U.S. It was designed to make a strong effort to correct what had already been documented, and to minimize, if not erase, the aura of fantasy around the Organization and its members. It was important to ascertain whether the written reports were indeed true or a product of anyone's or any particular office's agenda.

By far, the oral histories and interviews provided more clarity to what had been in doubt about the local Mafia. Besides providing explanations on the cultural and social customs among western Sicilians, they also included pertinent information on settlement and assimilation. In sum, while this methodology proved enriching and extremely valuable, the insights from each personal encounter were much more substantial than any history could produce.

• • • • • • • • •

Part I

The Earliest Mafiosi in the Philadelphia area

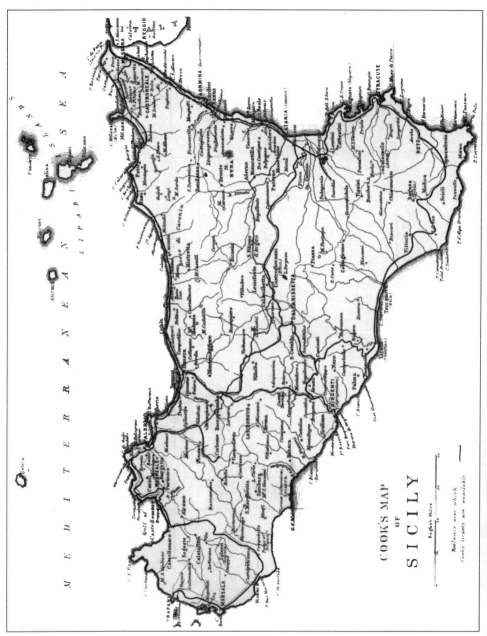

Map of Sicily from Thomas Cook's *Travels* (1899).

Sicilian Mafia networks
in the eastern half of Pennsylvania
●●

It was that aloofness.

And inside, "he who plays alone always wins" was ever present in these men's minds.

Individualists.

Guardians of the real and ideal, they maintained a degree of distance between themselves and those who were not a part of their honored society.

Mafiosi immigrants settled throughout the rural and urban areas of the Commonwealth of Pennsylvania by the end of the nineteenth century. The state's eastern half had concentrations of these men within the labor camps or burgeoning immigrant colonies. They came only from the provinces of Palermo, Trapani, Agrigento and Caltanissetta as young Mafiosi, initiated into the organization as teenagers. They had left Sicily and their parents' homes, but they returned often to finalize their past lives on the island or to remain there, disappointed in America.

3

It is difficult to link general conditions, political or otherwise, in Sicily with migrations to the United States at this time because Sicilians had left the island decades earlier for greater economic advantages in Louisiana. It is likewise doubtful that external influences from mainland Italy allowed for such migrations from mostly the area around the island's capital, Palermo and not other places on the island. A report on conditions in Sicily in 1876 by Leopoldo Franchetti and Sidney Sonnino found few changes on the island from the pre-unification years.[1] Denis Mack Smith wrote that travel, transportation and communications within Sicily in the 1880s and 1890s by land or sea were not only slow but the information often unreliable. What news about the United States was transmitted to Sicilians came usually from those that visited the U.S. and, overall, it was positive. Not that Sicily's government and the Italian politicians threatened the Mafia in western Sicily: In the 1890s, Italian Prime Minister Giovanni Giolitti reasoned that implementing reforms of any kind in Sicily was futile because the Mafia's influence there was indelible.[2]

But some young Mafiosi were restless and decided to see the U.S., if at first it was to be a temporary sojourn or to make names for themselves here. Documents and public records bear the names of young males from environments similar in topography to Sicily who first labored, then settled within Pennsylvania's borders. No one knows in what locale the Mafia members or Family were first established, despite that the Pennsylvania Crime Commission's 1970, 1980 and 1990 reports cited the "earliest" Mafia group in Luzerne County.[3] A descendant of one of these immigrant Mafiosi of the 1880s stated that his grandfather was like other newcomers who sought employment in mining or in the industrial and agricultural sectors in Pennsylvania's mountains. Montedoro, a village in the province of Agrigento released many of its residents to Pittston and

4

environs in Luzerne County, an area that resembled the sulfur mining regions in Sicily. Criminal activity however, was often part of overzealousness among the young males. Historian Thomas Pitkin reported that in these parts of Pennsylvania that many individuals of Sicilian ancestry participated in counterfeiting and had associations with others in New York as well as in Philadelphia by the 1880s.[4] It was a network with weak links to Philadelphia, however, since no reported Sicilians from Montedoro settled in the city to continue contact.

Counterfeiting in the 1880s and 1890s was not then considered a "Mafia" crime, or a crime associated with any specific group; but eventually Mafiosi in the U.S. did become involved in printing and passing fake currency. Nick Gentile, who migrated to the U.S. in 1903, and who

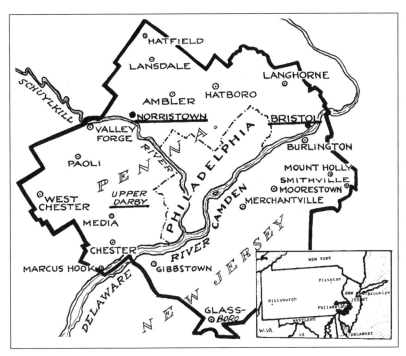

Map from 1930 shows locations of Mafia members and activity in and around Philadelphia.

was initiated into the Mafia in Philadelphia in 1906, confirmed that counterfeiting was long in practice among his fellow Friends. Gentile added that when he "became a man" in the Organization, "Don Piddu" Morello had been boss in New York but shortly afterwards was sent to a federal prison on counterfeiting charges.[5] His conviction, and that of Ignazio "Lupo" Saitta was enough to forestall other Friends from committing that crime again within their network.

A noteworthy account of the activities of the western Sicilians in Luzerne County showed a strong and continued contact with New York City's residents who were also from the mining areas in the province of Agrigento.[6] These contacts included non-Mafiosi but the reports only address criminal activities, which were then of public concern, not any other immigrant issue. If anyone from Agrigento's industry of mineral deposits and deep caverns went to Philadelphia, he and his activities are unknown. If this had not been the case, the city would have been cited earlier for an established Family venue.

Contemporaneous to Luzerne County's colonization, a group of young males from Sciacca, called by Mack Smith a "sizable town" in the 1870s,[7] arrived in Montgomery County in suburban Philadelphia. Primarily, industry, and the visual reminder of Sciacca in Norristown's terraced landscape rising from the banks of the Schuylkill River, attracted the Sciaccatani. But it was the land in the borough's east end that drew Sciacca's farmers here while its fishermen migrated to the harbors of New York and Boston. Farther west of Sciacca, Campobello di Mazara yielded a few adventurous young men to the area around lower Bucks County, near Bristol.[8] The second and third generations of these men knew the stories of initial struggles, not unlike others who left agrarian societies in Europe and who were asked to come for various purposes. Many young

6

Mafiosi came from farming backgrounds in western Sicily and most were middle-class, not of lower economic circumstances. They were usually taller, closer to six feet or over, than non-Mafiosi. Many came from towns, not villages. Opportunity, more than poverty, seemed to be the reason for so many young adult males to leave their parents' homes. Many returned. Some men were educated; others were not. Some left fianceés in Sicily, intending to bring them to the U.S. when a home could be made of a house. Some men had trades to fall back on, after spending years accumulating the finances for sole proprietorship. Among other Sicilian men in the fledgling colony, the Mafiosi were a minority.

At first, there were no connections between Mafiosi in the eastern part of Pennsylvania, or in the Philadelphia area, with the reputed "first" Mafia in the United States. Americans became acquainted with the word, "Mafia" when the major wave of immigration of Sicilians from Palermo, Sicily's capital, and its surrounding area had settled in New Orleans in the 1860s. It was in New Orleans, Louisiana that "the existence of such a society has been known and believed in by the public generally for a great many years," said New Orleans U.S. Attorney William Grant to the U.S. Attorney General William H.H. Miller in 1891.[9] Subsequently, some writers perceived the New Orleans "Family" was the "first" in the U.S. because many Mafiosi were included in the recruitment for labor. Actually, employment agencies from the U.S. went to Palermo, Monreale and neighboring towns seeking males, Mafiosi or not, to work in the lumber industry or in the manual labor work outside of the city on the plantations. Richard Gambino wrote that Sicilians were "far more efficient as laborers and less troublesome as people." They were the only whites to work the fields.[10]

It was perhaps New Orleans' strong nativism and anti-Italian sentiment that aroused the U.S. public's awareness

7

of the Mafia at this time. Compared to other states, Louisiana exploited ethnic bias, especially in its lynchings. Characterized by Gambino as "economically-motivated" because Sicilians rose faster in status than any other immigrant group, Louisiana's "Italians," (which included Sicilians), were second only to blacks as victims of vigilante justice. This was also true in Colorado, Mississippi, Illinois, North Carolina and Florida.[11] Thus, the Mafia became known widely in the U.S. when the "largest lynching in U.S. history," of ten males of Sicilian and one of Italian ancestry became the victims more of hysteria about the Mafia than any other reason. They were accused of having killed New Orleans Police Chief David Hennessey. The timeliness of the lynchings could be related to the Populist movement but, argued Roger Lane, "murder," which these lynchings were indeed, is not precipitated by "why...but where and when."[12] Mafia "killings" were unknown generally elsewhere in the U.S. and certainly any rumors of a Mafia in either the rural or urban areas never created the stir as in the South.

New Orleans' residents who originated from Palermo, Sicily, had one prominent link to a Montgomery County resident who was a member of the DiGiovanni Family[13] and who arrived in the early 1880s. He was called, "Zu Ninu"[14] and had fellow *paesani*, or those from his hometown in Sicily, blood relatives and not, in New York, New Orleans, Kansas City and then in suburban Philadelphia by way of his marriage to a woman from Sciacca. Among the notable names repeated in countless works on the eleven men lynched in New Orleans, the alleged "Mafiosi" were: Matranga, Provenzano and Macheca (correctly: Marceca), *paesani* of the DiGiovannis. "Zu Ninu" was an immigration broker, farmer, real estate investor and *padrone* of a sort. He held this position largely because of his literacy and his leadership skills within an immigrant colony outside of

8

Philadelphia that was almost entirely from western Sicily, and thus isolated from the mainland Italian groups from Abruzzi, Campania and Calabria. Other western Sicilian towns in Montgomery County, suburban Philadelphia, with ties to New York and New Orleans were Monreale, Caltabellotta and Calamonaci.

Evidence of Sicilian Mafiosi outside of Philadelphia is much stronger than any information supporting some Mafiosi activity within the city. The most significant proof of western Sicilian settlement is beyond Philadelphia's boundaries where a network system that was practiced by middle-class western Sicilians was in place by the 1880s. The network system probably originated in Sicily's medieval period. Economics, protocol, decorum and hierarchy were its primary concerns. Showing respect and honor in diverse forms was taught to females as well as to males. "Vossia," the formal address was used for those with titles, for those with seniority within the family, and for those in authority. A customary kiss of the hand usually followed. But respect and honor were by-products of the network founded on economics, which was the real basis for relationships, blood or non-blood.

The Great Migration Period allowed for the network system of a certain class and section in Sicily to become a tradition which distance would not disconnect. The western Sicilian middle-class was involved in networks for social, political and to further economic interests. Females, just as the males of this caste were subject to their tradition. Communicating interests through these networks involved every *paesani* colony in the United States. Pitkin noted one such network connecting the natives of Corleone with *paesani* in Chicago, New Orleans, New York and Pittston, Pennsylvania.[15] The absence of a western Sicilian colony within Philadelphia in the 1880s and 1890s indicates neither Mafia activity nor any network in which to connect to

The Mafia's stronghold in western Sicily is emphasized to show its remoteness from the rest of Europe.

the main base of operations in the U.S., in New York. The only links to New York at that time were arising from Luzerne or Montgomery County. Sciaccatani in Montgomery County formed a network with *paesani* in Boston, lower Manhattan (especially on Elizabeth Street) and in Brooklyn while the Palermitani's network joined New York and New Orleans with the suburban Philadelphians. The network system of middle-class western Sicilians did not identify yet solely with Mafiosi at this time, but it was a way in which the Mafia as an organization could use its native culture to develop and to expand within the United States.

The answer to Anton Blok's question on why western Sicilians had a Mafia is related to this system of continued communications. Blok wondered how "some other principle

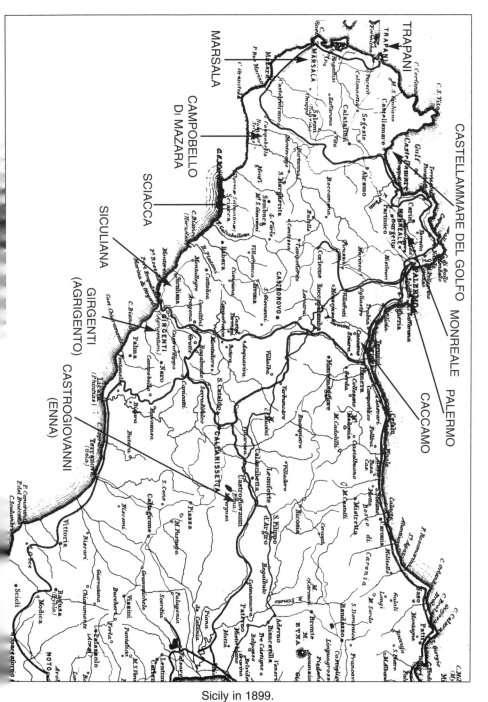

Sicily in 1899.
Western Sicily, the birthplace and base of the Mafia, with the towns referenced in text.

11

of organization structures human relationships in pervasive ways" and failed to realize, just as Marc Bloch, that mutual obligations and kinship among middle-class western Sicilians were bound by pecuniary means.[16] It was the force behind relationships and the network system. In the U.S., the networks were used to join mates and material assets between individuals of different colonies, to locate better employment, to find desired goods for sale or consumption, or to hide until trouble passed. In reality, there were many "kinships" an individual Sicilian could have had, and he could use them at will, just as any female. It was the mere potential of networks that Mafiosi realized, even at such distances that would make the Organization flourish.

There is no available information on the hierarchy of the first Mafia Families in New Orleans or in suburban Philadelphia that would establish relation in structure or in consanguinity to test the Families' desire for perpetuity. As for any details on the type of organization that these immigrant Sicilian Mafiosi in suburban Philadelphia had, the information is somewhat sketchy; but individuals who lived within the colony acknowledged that the Mafiosi did associate together. Francis A. J. Ianni in 1972 described his research on the Montgomery County Sicilians in the 1950s as his "first real contact as an anthropologist with Italian Americans in organized crime" and, he said he learned about several generations of these western Sicilians from the 1880s and 1890s. Basing his analyses on information gathered then from others, Ianni characterized his subjects as the "leading Sicilian American businessmen... All were related by blood or marriage." He further reported second-hand accounts on the "blood feuds" and the "intricate, overlapping kinship and business relationships among them." He perceived the Montgomery County Sicilians' main social unit was the family and that each family "made its own law and its men their own destiny."[17] (Refer also to Appendix I.)

This "introduction" did not allow Ianni to identify and to distinguish western Sicilian culture from the "southern Italian culture" he referred to generally, as well as specifically. But the suburban Philadelphians obviously led Ianni later to formulate his "Kinship and Social Control" theory in criminology that was repeated in his work on New York families with the same cultural roots. There may have been no more than six or seven Sciaccatani who were part of what Ianni erroneously called, "organized crime," (what was then a safe word to use in lieu of "Mafia" or "Syndicate"), but this terminology was legally without substance because none of the "leading businessmen" was involved in illicit activities. Sciaccatani in lower Manhattan and in Brooklyn, meanwhile, had aroused some interest with law enforcement by a few criminal incidents in which they were victims as well as perpetrators. In several instances, *The New York Times* reported on Black Hand and "Mafia" crimes on Elizabeth Street in lower Manhattan where primarily Sciaccatani resided alongside of Corleonesi. It was there that the Saitta ("Lupo")-Morello gang had its headquarters and an undisputed "Mafia" presence.[18] Nick Gentile, a Mafioso in the first decade of this century was more specific in naming the "sciaccatani," one of only a few identified western Sicilian groups, as "Mafiosi" in New York at this time.[19]

With regard to Philadelphia, again, the city had a secondary role in organized crime and the Mafia. In 1896, Secret Service agents were reported to have arrested in New York City a group which formed a counterfeiting network with "Italians in Philadelphia, Baltimore, Scranton, and other towns in the coal regions of Pennsylvania."[20] The Secret Service was also said to have pursued reputed Mafia activities in Philadelphia through 1903 in connection with other police in major U.S. cities,[21] but with insignificant findings. Identifying the Mafia was a difficult obstacle to

13

overcome. Evidently, there was no proof of a Mafia in Philadelphia at that time.

If one were seeking to verify the possibility that Sciaccatani and Palermitani and Monrealesi in suburban Philadelphia could have been members of the Mafia, there were some documented sources from Sicily in the 1880s and 1890s written by law enforcement and civilians alike. The former police chief of Palermo, Antonio Cutrera published his reports of several quasi-Mafia groups that operated in western Sicily in Agrigento, Monreale, Favara, Enna, Misilmeri, Bagheria and in Sciacca.[22] Cutrera claimed that these Mafia counterparts were all-male secret societies, had rules, initiation rites, exclusivity to members and included some references to the Roman Catholic Church. Combining these important elements, the western Sicilians in suburban Philadelphia, as in colonies elsewhere in the U.S. also had founded mutual beneficial societies, some dedicated to the Blessed Virgin Mary,[23] or to a popular Sicilian saint with initiation rites that are remarkably close to that used in the Mafia. They continue to the present.

Cutrera wrote that the "Mafia-like" group in Sciacca was "La Scattialora" and the one in Monreale was called, Stopagglieri,[24] (or in Sicilian, *stuppagghiari*.)[25] Originating from just outside the border of Palermo in Monreale and home to most of New Orleans' Sicilian population, the name, "stuppagghiari" was a derogatory term for a group first described in a Palermo trial in August of 1877.[26] Some of the defendants in this case testified in court about their initiation ceremonies that involved fingerpricking and the burning of a sacred image before fellow *compari* from Monreale. Giuseppe Montalbano calculated that "one hundred and fifty members" lived in that town in the 1870s.[27]

Diego Gambetta found some groups in western Sicily that were "parallel to the Cosa Nostra" and were active

SICILIAN GOATHERDS.

Examples of men who qualified as the Sicilian Mafia's strength
in previous centuries.

(FROM JOHN STODDARD'S *LECTURES — SICILY IN 1906*)

between Agrigento and Trapani called, *stidde,* Sicilian for
"stars."[28] He identified these early twentieth century groups
as "proto-Mafia." He conceded that the Mafia was native to
Sicily's western section but was in agreement with other
sociologists that the Mafia arose after 1860. Though the
historians and even some recent findings on medieval Sicily
point to a "proto-Mafia" more in the late Middle Ages, the
lack of criminal evidence to activities within Mafia
Families or with Mafiosi individually in the late nineteenth

15

century in the U.S. forces one to examine a cultural, non-criminal aspect that suggested more covert involvements among members. Some traditional Mafia activity did occur, although it may not be regarded as illicit. Some older Sicilian Americans spoke of "Zu Ninu," for example, and recalled him charging fees for his various services which included meeting and escorting immigrants from Ellis Island to Pennsylvania, finding employment for those seeking it and translating documents or orally in person. He also had a large outdoor oven for his neighbor's use for a fee—an accommodation that harkened back to the medieval period and the prestige of the hearth's owner. Impersonal crime, such as stealing from open railroad cars and any other unguarded commodities also were not beyond the reach of what the immigrants, including Mafiosi would do. However, the Luzerne and Montgomery County Mafiosi were found to initiate income-producing businesses as a priority in order to be independent, or, to have others become dependent upon the services or products. Within only a few years, the Montgomery County males identified as Mafiosi, (or to Ianni, "the leading businessmen") were self-employed in importing, manufacturing, local food sales, construction of houses and farming on their own land before the end of the nineteenth century.[29] Consequently, the economic mobility of these western Sicilians can be measured by in the considerable number of real estate holdings which, compared to other "Italian" groups, was quite suggestive. But were these successes to be attributed to the Mafia or Mafia associates? Ianni made no assumptions in writing but it was a known fact that "Zu Ninu" owned many large farms throughout the county and his fellow Mafiosi also owned a significant number of rental properties and businesses.

New Orleans' Sicilians had accomplished the same about a decade earlier: the city's mayor in 1890 had commented that "the Italians" (seventy percent of whom were of Sicilian ancestry) monopolized the local fish, produce and oyster industries.[30] Historian Christopher Duggan cited a source that estimated that "Italians" in New Orleans in the 1890s had nearly three thousand shops and numerous firms operating under their auspices.[31] Pitkin recounted the same prosperity among the Sicilians in New York City,[32] yet no evidence ever implied that the Mafia was at the root of the upward mobility of so many. But eventually, the Mafia's ties to wealth would soon become known more within a negative, or criminal, scope.

• • • • • • • • •

Philadelphia's early "Italian" crime
●●●

It is a fact of historical record that many immigrants from western Sicily were able to succeed materially as did many from mainland Italy without resorting to illegal means. Indeed, this information greatly diminishes any argument in favor of Daniel Bell's "Queer Ladder of Social Mobility" theory which claimed that economic disadvantages within the immigrant communities led many of its residents to participate in organized crime.[33] It was certainly not the case with the Mafiosi, but it was with many individuals whether they lived in ethnic colonies or not. It seemed to be a matter of character along with economic need that propelled many towards deviance and illegal activities. Though not to be construed solely as an artifact of any particular ethnic group, certain offenses became associated with all "Italians" by the early 1900s.

Perhaps the memories of the 1891 hangings and the hysteria of a "Maffia" looming in every place in the U.S. where any "Italian" resided were enough for the news media to dwell on the crimes suddenly occurring in immigrant colonies. A rising immigrant population in any city

18

allowed for developments of various social problems, among them criminal activities. However, by about 1900, after a generation of Italians and Sicilians intended to stay, their internal conflicts became newsworthy.

The Black Hand overshadowed all other "Italian" ethnic crime by its overt symbols—the inked handprint and letters sent with demands of certain amounts of money to be placed at a certain place and time. Unlike Sicilian Mafiosi, Black Handers, most of whom traced their ancestry to the region of Campania in mainland Italy, [34] usually informed their victims, or anyone, of who they were, either face-to-face or in their letters. Black Hand activity in Philadelphia and throughout Pennsylvania was documented timely in the press in the early part of the twentieth century. By that time, the word "Mafia" was used interchangeably with "Black Hand," because after the 1891 hangings, the Mafia's reputation degenerated into solely a criminal image,[35] and one that could be sensationalized in the press. Combining Cesare Lombroso's criminological theory that all criminals were generally underdeveloped humans, offenders were targeted in the popular press as well. The news media on both continents in the 1890s came to categorize "Italian crime" with the Black Hand and the Sicilian Mafia, thus applying the current racist views on what were termed by Lombroso as the new "atavistic" and "primitive" groups who left Europe for the U.S., the Sicilians and southern Italians.[36]

There were however, some instances in which the so-called "Black Handers" challenged the theory of racial inferiority attributed to southern Italians: when Black Hand extortions were reported to be common in areas without immigrant Italians. Such was seen in the western half of the Commonwealth of Pennsylvania in New Castle.[37] This case, and others noted in *The New York Times* also defied Nelli's generalization that the Black Hand was localized only in urban "Italian districts."[38] *The New York Times* published the names of offenders of non-Italian ancestry who used the Black Hand modus operandi: Walter Brannigan, Bernard Watts, John Gary and Michael Filesetor.[39] Other ethnic groups mimicked the Black Hand style of crime in extortion letters written in their native languages of German, Polish and Greek, and these were sent to those within their groups.[40]

By 1907, the Pennsylvania State Police promised to wage a "war against the Black Hand throughout Pennsylvania." By then, the Black Hand crimes included kidnappings, and sometimes murders to extract money from victims in Philadelphia as well as in lesser industrialized areas.[41] Bombings spread the word that some did not acquiesce to the Black Hand's requests. In 1910, one bomb in Philadelphia's "Little Italy" was set between the rowhouses located at 907 and 909 South Ninth Street. It shattered neighboring homes' windows, threw residents from their beds, but did not warrant enough fear from the letter's recipients to pay the "shakedown artists."[42] The Philadelphia Police Homicide records report on a few Black Hand-related deaths in 1914, and then in 1921 and 1922, but it is impossible now to link them with any Sicilian Mafia activity that may have been retributive. The last Black Hand homicide in Philadelphia seems incredible: in 1926, during Prohibition, and when the local Mafia was strong, someone was killed because his assailant wanted him "to join the black hands."[43] But even then, in the waning years of immigration, there was no western Sicilian colony or homogeneity within Philadelphia on a particular street or area for Mafiosi to claim as a living and working environment. With the territory of the Mafia less defined in Philadelphia, the seeds of non-conformity and vulnerability to external forces were thus sown. It was then in this broad expanse of area where the conservative Mafia tradition was

WINDOWS BROKEN BY EXPLODING DYNAMITE

SCENE OF ALLEGED "BLACK HAND" ATTACK

Dynamite placed on the ledge of a window, between the store of Michael Volte, at 909 S. 9th st., and that of Frank Marstale, of 907 S. 9th st., early this morning, shattered the windows of both properties, threw tenants of several houses out of their beds and created a "Black Hand" scare in the vicinity of 9th and Christian sts. According to Marstale, he received an alleged "Black Hand" letter several weeks ago, demanding $2,500 under penalty of death to himself and family.

(SOURCE: *EVENING BULLETIN*)

practiced in a more factious form. Few individuals then were less likely to have been able to identify Mafiosi in Philadelphia's "Little Italy" in South Philadelphia or in other neighborhoods because the Family was greatly outnumbered by eastern Sicilians and southern Italians, and because there was no contiguous physical "sanctuary" to establish a territorial setting for Mafia activities.

Ianni's anthropological research on the suburban Philadelphia western Sicilians found no parallels in other areas of Pennsylvania or within the city of Philadelphia with which to compare cultural differences. There were small colonies of western Sicilians in lower Bucks County from Campobello di Mazara and a few scattered families in

Philadelphia County from Castellammare del Golfo, the city of Palermo and environs, Caccamo, Enna, Agrigento and Caltanissetta in North, northwest and South Philadelphia, but none of these groups was large enough or as remarkable as the Montgomery County Sicilians during and just after the Great Migration Period.

The Italian ethnos generally did receive some attention in Philadelphia through the criminal justice system. Many interpretations could arise from the information. As studied and analyzed by historian Roger Lane, the late nineteenth century criminal records had "a somewhat inflated number of homicides charged to those with Italian names."[44] He figured that the ratio was "6.7 deaths per 100,000 Italian-born in Philadelphia between 1891 and 1900."[45] Lane presumed some fallibility with the police's record-keeping, perhaps recalling the influences of Lombroso, the Populists and others with anti-Italian attitudes in the 1890s. Actually, Lane was only partly correct— the cycle of criminal volatility within the Italian colony in Philadelphia was longer and relative to overall immigration growth from c. 1890 to c. 1920. In Philadelphia, the homicide records from the c. 1890 to c. 1920 period are remarkable for Italian-on-Italian killings during the height of the Great Migration: 85% of the victims with Italian surnames were found to have been slain by those also with Italian surnames.[46] Other Italian colonies in the U.S. seem to show the same rise in criminal activity paralleling the increase of the Italian immigrant population. For example, Nelli and Pitkin cited extraordinary internal conflicts among Italian groups in the major urban areas as well as in the rural mining towns where misdemeanors and felonies were commonplace.[47] It was at this time that the extortion wave began and was sensationalized by the news media, generally without reference to the Sicilian American Mafia.

Some of the Italian-on-Italian crime did, however, involve the Mafia. Nick Gentile, not yet a Mafioso when he arrived in New York from Sicily in 1903 related that his *paesani* watched over him, where he was staying and while he was employed, because Sicilians before him had been robbed by those of mainland Italian ancestry. Gentile summed up this time as when, "I was myself protected and I protected."[48] Neapolitans, Calabrians and Sicilians were victimized along with Abruzzesi and Baresi throughout the U.S. during this period of acclimation. However, this rough period has been perceived variously by others—what crimes arose seemingly from the stresses of assimilation in a new environment, or from human foibles, were interpreted as the "stepping stones" in financial gain for a few. Indeed, the Italian-on-Italian victimization cycle was hardly a justification for Bell's "Queer Ladder of Social Mobility" or any other theory which focussed on organized crime because the only organization at that time was clearly with the western Sicilians, no other group.

• • • • • • • • •

The Genesis of the Philadelphia Sicilian American Mafia

●●●

Before 1900, the Mafia, as it existed in and around Philadelphia, assumed few of the characteristics which have traditionally defined the Organization in purpose and function. Moreover, the Department of Justice's definition of organized crime had little relevance to the Mafia of this period: Organized Crime has a hierarchy of members organized to use violence and other illegal means to obtain profits.[49] Few Mafiosi in the U.S. in the late nineteenth and early twentieth centuries were involved in illegal enterprises or used violence to extort, if we were to believe the accounts about the New Orleans "Mafiosi." Gambino's research found all of the alleged "men of honor" in the Hennessey case to be employed legitimately with many who were self-employed. Gentile's accounts also verify many Mafiosi working and continuing to work legitimately in Pittsburgh, New York, Topeka and Cleveland just as he was going about from one (legal) job to another before 1920.[50] Although Philadelphia's Mafia Family at the turn of

24

the twentieth century had no written history on its members' activities to mark conformity with its counterparts in other places, there has been no evidence uncovered yet to suggest that the city's early Mafiosi were not employed legally.

There is evidence, however, on Philadelphia's early Mafia which is incidental. *The Philadelphia Inquirer* in 1903 had mentioned the possibility of a Mafia Family operating in Philadelphia based on the police report of one resident in South Philadelphia. In another incident, Magistrate Toughill held three "fine looking men...a type much above the Italian seen in the street and railroad laboring gangs" for threatening a woman that same year. But the magistrate's opinion was that the threats to the woman came from men in "an organization akin to the Mafia that was extorting money in Philadelphia's 'Little Italy'."[51] Gentile recounted a time when he was already known in Boston and in Chicago as a power to be reckoned with by the time he became initiated into the Mafia in Philadelphia when he was twenty-one years old. Unfortunately, the most important event in this Mafioso's life was not given further elaboration as to the circumstances in Philadelphia that made this city the venue for the initiation ceremony. Gentile was from Siculiana in the Province of Agrigento, a few miles west of the city of Agrigento on the island's coast. There were some immigrants from Agrigento in Philadelphia, but no information could be obtained as to confirm whether any were Mafiosi then, or later. Nonetheless, Gentile did claim that at the time he "became a man" in Philadelphia, "in each city of America these families had been forming" and in New York and Brooklyn, there were "two thousand" associates by 1906.[52]

There would have been enough Mafiosi in the Philadelphia area by about 1900 to form a Family, judging from the number of members who already were residing in

Largest
Circulation in
Pennsylvania

3, 1903 —Copyright. 1903, by The Philadelphia Inquirer Co.   WEATHER—Snow   ONE·CENT

SAY THEY HAVE UNEARTHED
MAFIA HAUNT IN "LITTLE ITALY"

Police in Making Raid on
Down-Town House Believe
They Have Found Branch
of the Society

Resident of the Quarter De-
clares He Was Threatened
With Violence Unless He
Paid Money

That a branch of the Mafia, the dreaded Italian organization, or some similar so-ciety, is in existence in "Little Italy," is the declaration of several Italians and the conviction of the police of the Sev-enth and Carpenter streets station house. As a result three Italians are now under arrest waiting the developments of fur-ther investigation. They are Fortunato Burgesi, Frank Lacanai and Salvator Ju-hana. The technical charge upon which they are held is carrying concealed deadly weapons.

About a week ago Michael Saine, a mid-dle-aged Italian, living at 522 Carpenter street, complained to the police that a band of men who had rooms in the rear of 808 Carpenter street had threatened him with violence unless he gave them $60. He gave them $20, he said, all the money he had, but when this was paid over, Saine says, and he attempted to leave he was forcibly detained and compelled to take an oath of secrecy and allegiance.
Police Raided House

COURT IN REAR OF 808 CATHERINE STREET
Cross shows house where police made arrests.

One of the earliest headlines on the local Mafia — from 1903.
(SOURCE: *PHILADELPHIA INQUIRER*)

the area. But it is difficult to determine if Philadelphia had
its own separate Family unit or was an appendage of a New
York Family. Philadelphia indeed was a Mafia site of activity but it is unknown if an independent Family could be justified. One Mafioso of the 1920s did claim that many bosses

lived mostly outside of Philadelphia in both the Pennsylvania and New Jersey suburbs. He did not know who was in the hierarchy but said that the Family was organized and interacted with New York. What was also revealed was that the Montgomery and Luzerne Counties' Mafiosi bypassed Philadelphia's Family and associated with those Mafia members in New York for social as well as political and economic reasons.

Philadelphia's *partiti*, or members, could claim widespread networks despite the slow communications existing around the turn of the twentieth century. The main impediment to these Sicilian American Mafiosi however, was that there was no substantial western Sicilian colony in Philadelphia with "men of honor" from the same town to form a solid foundation in this Family. Instead, Mafiosi from various towns in western Sicily had only the Tradition of the Honored Society, their language and foreign culture to keep them united and to maintain a Family as it would have been in Sicily. All of these factors though, were fated to weaken by continued exposure to American cultural influences. As a result, although Philadelphia's early Sicilian American Mafiosi were thinly spread in the city, suburban counties and south Jersey, a tradition of allowances developed for the Philadelphia Family that eventually caused more breakdowns to the original integrity of the Organization in this city than in other Mafia Families in the U.S.

Through all of the mystery of this early period in Philadelphia's Mafia, there were some documented crimes here that indicated the setting for the local Family and the community's development. The homicides, in particular, portray the immigrant and second generation Italian Americans' environment. Victims were intentionally killed, because "...they refused to join the Black Hand..." Or barroom brawls that began as extortion attempts resulted in

27

deaths. Then there were the ubiquitous "unknown persons" who wore the same type of coat and hat and would target men on Christian Street, the main street in Philadelphia's "Little Italy." These were the men who eluded law enforcement most. With others, tempers turned to fatalities in this area where arguments about World War I, card games' losses, depression or mental illnesses were the reasons for taking others' lives. The Sicilian Caccamese colony around Sixth and Carpenter Streets lost five individuals in seconds of a killer's fury. One address on Christian Street had three murders on two different occasions. In 1918, one man, the store owner, shot another man twice in the head, "...during a quarrel over card game..." In 1919, almost one year later, at 2:20 A.M., an apparent gang leader named, "Bruno Gaetano" and some other men shot the same store owner and an employee without motive. All escaped arrest.[53]

Some individuals in Philadelphia did live in the first years of the twentieth century with one of the Mafia's tell-tale signs. Here, as in other areas of Mafia activity, some individuals bore the *sfregio*. Henner Hess reported that these *sfregi* "are so typically mafioso," although he also found that these cuts across the faces of Mafia traitors were used against unfaithful wives as well.[54] The Philadelphia Police had noted several males who were wanted for arrest and were to be identified by a "face scare[sic] on left cheek with skin drawn on scar" in 1909. One fugitive had a "scar on the left eye," (1913) while another "has a scar under left eye running to the Mouth." (1914)[55] Although it was not known where the *sfregi* were inflicted, these men in Philadelphia were the living witnesses to Mafia revenge.

Philadelphia's Sicilian American Mafia was able to be sustained through neighborhood interactions and mobility because it was, to some degree, organized. Henner Hess and many in law enforcement have tried to compartmen-

28

talize the Sicilian American Mafia and La Cosa Nostra into the "organization" or "syndicate" niche, but this evolving entity was unique to its inception, development, environment and cultural influences. The Mafia did have members, associates, (i.e., individuals who assisted the members), regulations, hierarchy, meetings, strategies and goals. Mafiosi also went by a behavioral code that was predictable. One early piece of evidence of the early U.S. Mafia's organizational structure came from William J. Flynn, a former Secret Service agent in the late nineteenth and early twentieth centuries. In his book, *The Barrel Mystery* (1919), Flynn documented information particular to Mafia networks and organizations throughout the U.S.: upon the arrest of Giuseppe (Joseph) Morello in 1909, (the same individual who was involved in counterfeiting), Flynn found written communications linking Morello with Vito Cascio Ferro in Palermo, Sicily, to Vincenzo Moreci in New Orleans and to an individual in the "Chicago gang." Morello, from Corleone, had murder charges dismissed in Sicily reputedly because of the Mafia's collusion with local law enforcement.[56] Pitkin also noted that Flynn, probably unintentionally, reported on the seniority of the New York Mafia Families and their influence on other Mafia Families in the U.S.: "Some of the [Morello] correspondence concerned the admittance into the Chicago branch of the society of a man questioned by the leaders in New York, who put the responsibility for his admittance up to the Chicago gang."[57] Here, Flynn suggested the existence of the five New York Families' roles over other Mafia members in the U.S. as well as the international and interstate activities that would have bound these men together in an organized state before 1909.

Philadelphia's Mafia Family in the early twentieth century already had the promise of failure, with no western Sicilian colony, with members allegedly from various Mafia

Christian Street in Philadelphia's "Little Italy" neighborhood at the beginning of the 20th century.

towns in Sicily living at a distance, and with no strong ties to New York. But there was another important fact about Philadelphia's Family—no one seemed to want to ensure the Family's growth by intermarrying with another from other Mafia groups, especially with the controlling members in New York. Unbound by any tie, Philadelphia stood in a position to dissolve. But apparently, there were some activities that were economically sound and which kept Philadelphia's Family an interest to the dominant Families.

Much of the respect paid to the New York axis powers by Philadelphia was apparently in material form and from one of the more consistent Family businesses—paid protection. Cooperation with law enforcement was a traditional practice between Mafiosi and police in Sicily, depending on the circumstances. That some Mafiosi were arrested in the late nineteenth century meant that many cases were not compromised; others were. It was possible that some Mafiosi in Sicily did not have any means to lift penalties, whereas the *alta*, or upper, Mafiosi in the professional classes did. Economic strata often determined how and if the *bassa*, or lower, Mafiosi would be able to evade convictions. The *bassa* Mafiosi though, had the continual problem of distinguishing themselves from the common criminals in such matters because of the Mafia's all-encompassing secrecy or *omertà*. Nonetheless, Gentile confirmed that "in the U.S., as in Sicily, the Mafia cooperated uninterruptedly with the police against bandits and gangsters, unauthorized to the extent of obtaining an exchange of a certain area of respect for same."[58] Thus, Mafiosi were distinguished from "bandits and brigands" in the U.S. and were not a part of a "syndicate" as argued by Joseph Albini or the "organized criminals" of Donald Cressey's later subjects.[59] Mafiosi in the U.S. could not, at that time, exhibit any non-law-abiding behavior and win favor with the local police.

The mere desire to organize men to protect residents within a community and to maintain order demonstrated that the Mafia's priorities in the U.S. were for a type of social stabilization and control that was practiced in western Sicily. This behavior also negated the parasitic quality which would describe the Black Hand and other loosely organized gangs of the same period who were non-conforming and deviant.

There is significance to be gleaned from the void in the Philadelphia Police's criminal records on these early Sicilian American Mafiosi. Corruption aside, there is a suggestion that police inaction can be understood as the recognition of a common interest in the community's welfare and in maintaining civil order. Nick Gentile, never denying his later involvement in narcotics activities, admitted that there was a time when immigrant Sicilians needed protection from Neapolitans and Calabrians within the ethnic enclaves throughout the U.S. from about 1905 to 1920.[60] Joseph Bonanno of New York also supported the Mafioso's role in assisting those in adversity during those years.[61] Without any attempt to be self-serving, these "Men of Honor" of long lives within the Organization portrayed a Sicilian American Mafia as an evolving group, eventually quite different in later years than the one they knew in their early adulthood.

The same absence of criminal records traceable to Mafiosi in the late nineteenth and early twentieth centuries is also found in Montgomery and Bucks Counties where the socio-economic mobility was noted. Although contemporary public reports, such as the newspapers, describe the Mafia as a feared criminal group and "dreaded Italian organization", the oral histories of these Mafiosi's descendants collectively explain why there were few, actual confirmed arrests of these men anywhere in the U.S.: integration within U.S. society, and lacking suspicion into areas of deviant behavior and criminal activities. Either few individuals were aware of anything unusual transpiring, or no one was victimized to the extent of notifying law enforcement. It should also be added that if anyone did do anything harmful to a Mafioso, his family, to members or to the colony in general, he was usually spoken as one who "went away."

Bloodless acts, in the Mafia tradition, incidentally, also meant exile.

• • • • • • • • •

In retrospect, in the approximate forty years before Prohibition, the Sicilian American Mafia and Mafiosi thrived in and around Philadelphia. Their presence, unveiled now, disputes many previously-held beliefs about early Italian and Sicilian colonies in Pennsylvania. Invariable as the Sicilian American Mafiosi's interactions were with other Italian regional groups in the same general areas, these "Men of Honor" from a subculture of western Sicily barely dented Philadelphia's and its suburbs' sparse and uneven record of underworld activities of those from among its lower social stratum. Collectively as an ethos, Philadelphia's Italians in review had achieved numerous gains since the time when immigrants from northern Italy migrated to the city well before the American Civil War. Some fought for the Union's cause. Some founded the first Italian national church in the U.S. in 1852. These northern Italians also may have paved a path in business and in some levels of society for many from southern Italy and Sicily,[62] despite regional differences. The city's business directories list several importing firms, macaroni factories, and various stores owned by those of Italian or Sicilian ancestry before 1900 and before the appearance of a Mafia. In the 1890s many employment agencies, factories and construction businesses purposely sought southern Italians and Sicilians for work. In Philadelphia, ethnic intimidation and discrimination by the native-born and "Americans" were not, in fact, as great a detriment to progress and integration for the Italian and Sicilian immigrants as internal conflicts within the immigrant neighborhoods with the often abusive *padroni* and Black Handers. Beginning with the commission of "Captain Joe" Malatesta in 1884, there was a remarkable number of Philadelphia policemen and detectives to try to control criminal activities, some investigating the Italian-on-Italian crime.

Putting to rest some long-held views that have been accepted as fact, it becomes clear that oversimplifications have dominated twentieth century academic thought on the Mafia, organized crime, studies on Italian and Sicilian immigrants and their areas of assimilation and acculturation. Moreover, for whatever reasons the criminologists and sociologists may have to affect their theories on specifically, the Sicilian American Mafia, there is an obvious tendency to taint such theories with conjectures, and to ignore facts. Early endeavors to provide frameworks or to craft a kind of model in which to explain the genesis of the Mafia in the U.S. are subject to the time in which "Mafia" and "organized crime" were considered synonymous. This work does not propose that the Sicilian American Mafia was defined as an example of organized crime: there is no record that the group was founded upon criminal activities. This work does however, provide what my research has uncovered to dispute previous claims to the contrary concerning Philadelphia's Mafia and its members. In particular, the "Queer Ladder of Social Mobility" and "Ethnic Succession" theories of the Mafia's roots in the U.S. are unsubstantiated with the data obtained regarding serious offenses in Philadelphia's "Little Italy" during the period from 1892 to 1919. It is worth repeating the Philadelphia Police's homicide record on one hundred and thirty-five (135) killings

34

from this period that involved either the perpetrator or victim of Italian or Sicilian ancestry.*

— 5 non-Italian-on-Italian cases;
— 7 Italian-on-non-Italian cases;
— 8 "unknowns"-on-Italian cases; and,
— 115 Italian-on-Italian cases.

Even with a slight variation in the numbers, the statistics are too meaningful to pass. Yet, with the record, the police's data and statistics and the circumstantial evidence of the Sicilian American Mafia's existence in Philadelphia and environs, there still were assumptions about whether the Organization was present and active. More troubling in recent years however, are prevailing traditions in academia that continue without dispute. To wit, there is Potter & Jenkins' work which contends that there was no Mafia in Philadelphia until the 1950s, after the Jewish Mob declined in power.[64] Then in late 1999, criminologist Nikos Passas publicly claimed that "discrimination, poverty and language barriers...push Italian Americans towards organized crime,"[65] on explaining the American Mafia's genesis.

Needless to say, the Mafia, LCN and organized crime still arouse more emotional responses than logical ones, or ones based upon fact. The history of Philadelphia's Mafia has a history then within itself of attempts to mask, to sabotage, to misrepresent the facts and to suspend attitudes and perceptions. The next part will examine the continuation of these traditions in another form, when identities become known and relationships, networks and conflicts have broader significance beyond the ethnic colonies.

• • • • • • • • •

_____
*This is based on their names and places of birth where noted on the records.

• •

Part II

Salvatore Sabella:
The First Known Boss of
The Philadelphia Mafia

• •

"Don Turiddu"

●●●●●●●●●●●●●●●●●●●●●●●●●●●●●●●●●●●●●●

He was Philadelphia's earliest leader who was known by name possibly because he lived when communications, the media and law enforcement began to notice the Mafia. At least publicly through the law.

But they had it all wrong then: Sabella was not the first Mafia boss of Philadelphia.[1]

"There were many bosses here before Salvatore Sabella," said one of his soldiers. Their marks were left in the most populous areas of Pennsylvania. Early in this century for example, merchants at the 9th Street "Italian Market" in South Philadelphia used to pay the Sicilian American Mafia to protect them against the Black Handers or Camorristi or other gangsters who made them prey. "With the Mafia...at least they gave you somethin'...the other gangsters gave you nothin' each time you paid them somethin'," reported one shopkeeper whose prominent store on 9th Street was a local enterprise before 1910. Many storeowners today still recall how in their youth they had experienced dynamite blowing out the store fronts of those whom extortionists victimized. Some businesses' walls still have bullet holes under formica veneers. It was part of identifying which stores did not pay the gangsters who "shook them down." Of course, the merchants could have paid "the Sicilians," as they were simply known, to protect them. They were not yet called, "Mafiosi"—at least not outright—it was too taboo among themselves. Some businessmen on 9th Street did however, pay "the Sicilians" to protect them and were grateful to these men of whom they knew so little. In fact, 9th Streeters were so appreciative to these Sicilians that when a Mafioso died, the Market mourned by closing its stores, even during typically busy shopping days. Some stores hung black sashes across windows and doorways.

This is what they used to call respect.

And it was reserved only for these Sicilian Mafiosi.

Most storekeepers at the prominent market in Philadelphia's "Little Italy" had not been aware that a fellow businessman and neighbor had been the local Mafia's *rapprisentanti,* the name formerly used for the leader of this group. Salvatore Sabella had been a known and respected storekeeper in Philadelphia since about 1914.[2] In the 1920s, he had an oil and cheese store which he co-owned with his brother-in-law, Leonard. He had also run a café during Prohibition called the "Third Ward Republican Club"[3] where soft drinks and pastries were sold to front the illegal activities of the men.

As of this writing, many individuals still recall "Don Turiddu," but few realize his importance as head of Philadelphia's Mafia Family from about 1919 to about 1931. Yet, his life had been misunderstood possibly because he retired as an active Mafioso by age forty and lived through the tenures of the next five bosses of Philadelphia. In fact, Sabella outlived two of the bosses who succeeded him, to be the oldest ex-boss of Philadelphia during Angelo Bruno's reign.

40

Sabella's Evolution as a Mafioso.
● ●

Salvatore Sabella's life began in western Sicily, the birthplace of the Mafia. The landscape can be frightening on this island with the deep valleys and individual heaps of rock that are called mountains. Some areas rest over earthquake zones while others vibrate from immature volcanoes. Salvatore Sabella was born of this natural environment near the gulf over which a Muslim castle still stands, hence the name, Castellammare del Golfo, his hometown or *paese*. Castellammare is charming, but isolating in the way in which its semi-circular harbor swings around the coast. Beyond the hills above the coast were other towns similarly settled in the past by Muslim groups and France's people from Normandy and Provence who brought their feudal culture to these parts of the island. Like the other nearby towns, it was a place where the Mafia was not unknown.

In the year that Salvatore Sabella was born, 1891, the Mafia was acknowledged as the more stable form of rule with Mafia influence in law enforcement, politics, trade and domestic economics. The Sicily of Sabella's youth was able

Castellammare del Golfo, Sicily.

(PHOTO BY AUTHOR)

to be recounted in history unlike in the previous century with literature that was perhaps more negative, but indicative of a place and people that were at best, provincial. Franchetti and Sonnino's 1876 study noted the differences between western and eastern Sicily.[4] Criminologist Cesare Lombroso likewise found in the 1880s and 1890s that geographic divisions on the island had ethno-cultural bases for separate ideologies.[5] Marxist views may have gained some currency on mainland Italy, but in Sicily, it was common knowledge that the Mafia influenced the Sicilian Parliament.[6] One *London Times* account of 1891 described the islanders as "deceitful, reticent, malicious and vindictive...owing to the spirit of 'Mafia' and 'omerta'."[7] The remoteness of Castellammare may have spared its residents the exposure to any pejoratives from the latest group of *fuoristieri* (foreigners) who tried to reckon the Mafia's existence and purpose in western Sicily. But as two lawyers from Palermo and Messina wrote in their book, *Mafia*, "...for the Sicilian, [the Mafia] is a virtue: it is his glory."[8]

Sabella's family was not among the more prominent ones in Castellammare, but they also were not from the lower classes. He was raised as other boys in his class, given an opportunity to receive enough formal schooling to learn how to read, write and to do the necessary math to earn a living. Salvatore's father, John, and mother, Rosa then arranged for their son to be an apprentice in an occupation that would carry him into adulthood. For the young Salvatore Sabella, work in the slaughterhouse would determine his fate.[9]

It is unclear what circumstances would have allowed an employer to be physically abusive to a fourteen year old boy, but Salvatore Sabella afterwards admitted to long-term abuse at the hands of a man whom his parents obviously did not know would influence their son's life more than they did. One day in 1905, unable to withstand the beatings in the slaughterhouse, Sabella the young butcher, struck back and killed his employer. He was arrested later as an adult and from July of 1908 spent the next three years in a prison thousands of miles from his family in Milan, Italy.[10]

By the time that Sabella was released from prison, the Mafia became more newsworthy in Sicily as well as in the U.S., except that the Mafia became equated with the Black Hand. In the beginning of 1909, after spending years investigating "Italian" crime in New York, the police's Italian Squad's Lieutenant Joseph Petrosino met his death in Palermo, Sicily. Petrosino made many rigorous attempts to control Black Hand activities in New York and may have unknowingly threatened Sicilian Mafiosi there. When Petrosino continued his fact finding on suspected members of the Black Hand and Mafia in Sicily, he wrote down the names of known Mafiosi on the island. The last entry of names was "Vito Cascio Ferro born in Sambuca Zabut, resident of Bisaquino, Province of Palermo, dreaded criminal."[11] Yet, the Sicily that Sabella temporarily left had seemingly grown stronger with the Mafia and others which included Raffaele Palizzuolo, a Mafia boss and member of the Italian Parliament, Cascio Ferro's political allies and Giovanni Giolitti, then the Italian Prime Minister.[12] It was the Mafia which controlled the western part of the island and managed to quell the common offender while keeping anyone from mainland Italy in submission. In the 1890s to the 1900s, there were Mafiosi in every class, wrote Mack Smith.[13] It was the "Golden Age" of the Mafia "when non-legal violence became a recognized method of defending landowners and new property rights against the peasantry," reported historian Martin Clark.[14] Moreover, Mack Smith added that at this time that "Sicilian politicians would fight hard against any attempt at forcible suppression of boss politics and the mafia."[15]

It is likely that despite this climate that was favorable to Mafiosi that Sabella chose the United States rather than Sicily because his family was apparently not one of the elite Mafia families in Castellammare. It was sometime in 1912 that Sabella arrived in New York and made his way to the Castellammarese colony in Brooklyn. A short time later, he was in Philadelphia with his two brothers. They were a part of the network among Castellammaresi tying their native town in Sicily with *paesani* colonies in Brooklyn, Buffalo, Detroit and Philadelphia. And in each colony there were Mafiosi.

There is no information on whether Philadelphia's Mafia Family in the early century was originally Castellammarese or whether Sabella was the first boss in Philadelphia who was from Castellammare del Golfo. However, there is evidence that some Castellammaresi settled in Philadelphia before 1900 in the city's north and northwestern sections and that these Sicilians had limited contact with the Sicilians in South Philadelphia. But these

Castellammaresi do not seem to parallel chronologically with other Sicilian Mafia Families who had arrived earlier.

The disbursement of Sicilian colonies in Philadelphia would have been due to economic and cultural differences. The South Philadelphia Sicilians were mostly from the Province of Messina in the east; smaller groups from the western provinces of Palermo, Caltanissetta and Agrigento were already exposed to the Mafia tradition unlike the former from the island's eastern part. There also was rather uneven immigration from Sicily, as previously stated, with no substantial western Sicilian colony within Philadelphia to claim Mafiosi.

While in Philadelphia the Castellammaresi were a minority, in New York, they gained some notoriety by way of crime. Detective Michael Fiaschetti of the New York City Police's Italian Squad provided this information on some of Sabella's *paesani* who were also separately identified from other Sicilians. Fiaschetti wrote of some Castellammaresi Mafiosi as a Family, as murderers and as "talkers" early in the 1920s. One Castellammarese, Bartolomeo Fontano confessed to the killing of his *paesano*, Camilio[sic] Calazzo, as did his fellow vocal Mafiosi. Their "gang" had told them to end Calazzo's life—his body was later found in a sack in New Jersey. Afterwards, Fontano admitted to other Castellammaresi murders, spanning years which took place in several cities.[16]

It will never be known now if Sabella was made a member of the Mafia in New York or in Philadelphia. Although New York seems to be a more probable place where Sabella might have become recommended to the Organization among more of his own *paesani*, his new home in Philadelphia likewise could have been the venue of his "becoming a man." How Sabella was chosen and groomed to be Philadelphia's *rapprisentanti* or *capo*, the head of the family, remains speculative at best, but he had at least one advantage which many members of his Family did not have later, such as growing up in the western Sicilian culture where respect and honor were incorporated in every social aspect of one's life. Sabella may have been therefore, a Mafioso for no more than about five years when he was elevated to the highest position in the local hierarchy.

To be sure, Sabella's relationships with the New York Sicilian American Mafiosi established his place as *capo* of the Philadelphia Family before he was yet thirty years old. But Sabella's age is not of issue here; Philadelphia's Family's ancillary status is. It was already a Family with developmental problems because there were members in the Philadelphia area who were not of Mafia families in western Sicily. Even worse, local Mafia members from eastern Sicily had to be taught as adults about the basics of respect and honor before they could understand the traditional codes and customs of the Mafia.

One FBI report mentioned "Giuseppe Traina" of New York as the individual responsible for Sabella's ascendance in Philadelphia. Giuseppe, or Joe, Traina could have met Salvatore Sabella in either Philadelphia or in New York. He legitimately owned the Empire Yeast Company in New York and sold his product to several local businessmen in Philadelphia's "Little Italy." Another FBI witness report clarified Traina's status as of 1964 as "84 years old" and inactive within the Organization.[17] Nick Gentile described "Don Giuseppe" Traina (or "Don Pidduzzu") as the "substitute" of the powerful Toto D'Aquila, once considered a *"capo dei capi"* in New York.[18] Surprisingly, Traina's level of authority among the Friends still had others referring to him by his nickname, *lu viddanu* (the peasant).[19] Bonanno was less critical of Traina: he is first named as a member of the "clan" of Al Mineo (Manfredi), "an avowed ally of Joseph

46

Masseria's," then as an "early defector" along with Frank Scalise, of that clan.[20]

Traina was one of those quiet Mafiosi often termed a "sleeper"— someone in the Organization who is active enough to be respected and known, but passive enough not to draw the attention of law enforcement and the jealousy of others. He was a legitimate businessman, as other traditional "Men of Honor" were and played a transient part in the Mafia's activities that were noteworthy. That Traina was selected to "substitute" for someone called, "il terribile"[21] Toto D'Aquila speaks for itself. Traina was evaluated by D'Aquila. And Traina evaluated Sabella.

"Recommended" is the word used by Mafiosi to describe the first step in the process of "making" a member. At the time of Sabella's initiation, qualification was not contingent upon participation in murder or how well a thief one was. However, one was expected to kill upon command from the local hierarchy or to be able to kill another member with authorization by the Mafia bosses in New York.

Mafiosi managed to remain unnoticed in mainstream society in the Philadelphia area, so it is not unusual that Sabella's early life in the U.S. as a Mafioso eluded law enforcement. There is no evidence of Sabella's first years in New York or in Philadelphia to prove that he ever aroused law enforcement's attention, so we have no official record of what activities he participated in or how he evolved in crime to be selected as the Philadelphia *capo*. This was usually not the case in other large metropolitan areas in the U.S. or where western Sicilian colonies were located. U.S. law enforcement's general indifference to crime within ethnic enclaves seemed more evident in Philadelphia than in other cities where careful record-keeping produced information as to the handling and dispensation of criminal cases of alleged Mafiosi. The misspellings in most of the existent criminal records in Philadelphia, as well as the overall negligent recordings in the criminal indices, show a rather unaggressive approach to bringing cases to convictions. Perhaps the offenders left the city; or perhaps law enforcement did not have the means to investigate as they do today. What is certain is that many, many crimes were unreported because of political pressure, indifference and some collusion with the local Mafiosi, said those involved on both sides of the law.

Accordingly, if discretion could best characterize Philadelphia's Sicilian American Mafia before Sabella, as well as with Sabella's Family, it was to the Mafiosi's advantage, but a loss to history. No crime books or criminal histories ever mentioned Philadelphia's Mafia or Sabella during Prohibition, one of the most bloody, crime-ridden periods in the city. Yet Sabella was part of this underworld subculture that coexisted in Philadelphia along with scores of gangs, ethnic and non-ethnic, evading local law enforcement, internal warfare and competing mobsters.

The written history of the 1920s in Philadelphia also disqualifies this Sicilian American Mafia as "organized crime" because although the Family was organized, the purpose of its existence was not to gain profits through illegal means, except if one considered bootlegging as criminal. Harry Riccobene, initiated into Sabella's Family in 1927 said that "loan sharking, bootlegging and paid protection" were the only "illegal" incomes at this stage in the local Family's development. Joseph Bonanno, an admitted "Mafia Traditionalist" would later confirm that his *paesani*, his Friends and his "Tradition, in its pure form, shuns prostitution, narcotics peddling, extortion and kidnapping. These are considered unmanly activities."[22]

It took decades to fear the Mafia in Philadelphia's "Little Italy" neighborhood. Few knew what the Mafia was;

48

others were aware of some Sicilians who knew how to handle certain situations within the colony in ways in which others could not. There were some other Sicilians in Philadelphia who were involved in homicides in 1919 and were never apprehended by the police even though their names appeared in the records. These were the men who "'went away"—to prison, to Sicily or to death. No one was supposed to be more definitive. And no one dared to ask further.

Considering the demographics, the number of homicides in Philadelphia's "Little Italy" just within about four blocks on or around Christian Street was high: in 1918, there were 17 homicides, but not all because of the Mafia or other criminal groups; 13 homicides in 1919; and 10 killings in 1920.[23]

When Sabella became Philadelphia's Mafia leader, his responsibilities did include overseeing the loan-sharking, paid protecting and maybe robberies and thefts that were intercounty and interstate operations, all of which were highly lucrative, steady incomes. Crimes that had minimal personal interaction were also favored by Mafiosi such as stealing from stockpiled materials or products that could be sold for cash—hence, the need for the "junkmen" who were valuable associates.

The first years of Sabella's rise to *capo* or *rapprisentanti* were marked by a crisis, some setbacks and then a turning point in his life. The years, 1918 and 1919 saw the flu epidemic take away so many Philadelphia residents that the dead in coffins were piled high and left on street corners for the flatbed trucks to take them away. It was said that as soon as a sick person felt cold and unconscious, he or she was immediately removed from where they were and then laid in a coffin. These years were also when

49

Philadelphia's top Mafioso was deeply in love and ready to settle down to marriage and a family of his own.

When Salvatore Sabella first saw the teenage Maria Galante, he was smitten, said his children. She was Castellammarese, from what Sicilians called, *'na bona famigghia* ("a good family") with many Mafiosi. They seemingly had a few common interests but Salvatore was ten years older than his proposed fiancée and had to wait for her to be of age to marry. Maria's father soon signed his consent for his daughter to marry the most powerful Mafioso in Philadelphia. They would live the beginning of their lives together in "Little Italy."

Sabella, as a bachelor, was a member of St. Mary Magdalen de Pazzi Roman Catholic Church and lived alone. He was not a particularly religious man and not as known in his generosity towards the church as others in his group. He was quiet, never raising suspicions among his own or to outsiders. He worked at his legitimate and illegitimate jobs diligently. And he cared little to impress others of his stature, power and influence with Philadelphia's police, politicians and other local civil servants.

What Sabella encountered in Philadelphia's "Little Italy" was nothing less than the same types of conflicts among eastern and western Sicilians and every regional group from mainland Italy. As Pitkin had concurred, "Obviously there was no love lost between peninsular Italians and Sicilians"[24] and to a certain degree, Sabella and his Mafiosi met these challenges within provincial Philadelphia's more isolated ethnic colony in South Philadelphia. A more complex dynamic, involving economics or a particular class mentality may have been the reason behind the many conflicts within Philadelphia's "Little Italy." By the 1920s, with a cash flow emanating from primarily the bootlegging industry, class divisions were also

"JUST OFF THE BOAT!"
County Detectives Patsy Coco and Tony Waldron are shown examining liquor seized in a raid in a central-city building by county detectives.

(PUBLIC LEDGER)

noted in the values of the middle-class versus those of the lower class. It was evident in the parishioners of St. Mary Magdalen's who distanced themselves from those who attended Our Lady of Good Counsel Church, the other Italian national church one block away. And it was obvious that few from St. Mary Magdalen's patronized the Christian Street and Ninth Street street vendors or had businesses there among the newly arrived and working poor.

Nevertheless, shortly after they married, Salvatore and Maria moved close to where the paid-protection clientele and his cheese and oil store were, near the 9th Street "Italian Market." In just one year, a son was born. Then, within seven years, Maria would bear five more children during Prohibition, a time when her husband was home at unpredictable times.

• • • • • • • •

51

In the Public's Shadow during Prohibition
● ●

When the Volstead Act, or "Prohibition" was enacted,
Sabella, as those Mafiosi in New York, quickly became
involved in the illegal manufacture and sale of alcohol. One
of Sabella's soldiers, Harry Riccobene said that "Judges and
lawyers and politicians...they knew who (in the Mafia) to
contact" for their liquor which sold for multiple times more
to the Main Line Protestants than to South Philadelphia
rowhouse residents. Publicly it was Max "Boo Boo" Hoff
and Mickey Duffy who drew the news media to their misdeeds in the underworld with the Lanzetti brothers linking
the Italian ethnos to the same. Sabella and his Family however, were in the background during most of Prohibition.
Almost.

Philadelphia's "Little Italy" in the early 1920s was not
without some contact from those in the new Fascist form of
government in Italy, fascism was not of interest to Sabella,
but Fascist activities did inadvertently involve the local
boss and expose him criminally. According to Richard
Varbero, opinions about Fascism among Italians in
Philadelphia varied and often were met with violent

52

results. Varbero's one 1975 study of the South Philadelphia community's responses to Mussolini's reforms mentioned an incident by "Fascist sympathizers" ending in the bombings of some prominent Italian Americans' residences.[25] However, there are several versions as to what happened, aside from Varbero's conclusion. One day in 1923, Salvatore Sabella was arrested for what may have actually been another source of revenue for the local Family, besides profits from alcohol sales. The Philadelphia *Evening Bulletin's* story about the bombing at the Maggio's store at the 9th Street "Italian Market" tried to link that incident to a previous bombing at C.C.A. Baldi's home in Roxborough. Fascist sympathizers were suspected in both bombings. Baldi was believed to be a supporter of Mussolini; the owner of the property now in question, Michael Maggio, denied Fascist membership. When asked by the detectives about the bombing, Mr. Maggio said, "It is all a great mystery to me."[26] *The Philadelphia Inquirer* and *Public Ledqer*, meanwhile, dismissed any "Fascist" reference and directly blamed "the Black Hand."[27] These accounts would imply that the two men apprehended by the police at about 1 A.M. were the usual suspects in the frequent bombings in and around the Italian Market. Mr. Maggio, nevertheless, insisted that the police release the men, and himself posted $1,500.00 in bail for each individual. These alleged bombers were "distant relatives and meant no real harm," Mr. Maggio told the Magistrate. The police then released Friend Giuseppe Giorgesti[sic] of Bridgeton, New Jersey and Salvatore Sabella, the godfather of Maggio's son, Peter who had been born in 1920.[28]

• • • • • • • • •

By 1926 the Sabella family changed residences for the quiet suburbs where the Sabella children would be spared the frequent public shootouts by gangsters such as the

WHERE BOMB BLAST DAMAGED STORE

This shop window at 918 S. 9th St. was smashed among others in the neighborhood when the explosion occurred at 1:15 A.M. today. Nearby houses were rocked. Two men were arrested.

— EVENING BULLETIN

Lanzettis who made their reputations in and around "Little Italy's" busy streets. Stores like Cucinotta's Grocery, just north of the "wildest intersection," 9th and Christian Streets, had to replace its front windows several times a month because of stray bullets.[29] Gangsters shot on foot, from roaming vehicles, even from rooftops at 9th and Christian in a "War for Supremacy between South

Philadelphia's Narcotic Peddling and Bootlegging Gangs" in the 1920s.[30]

The crossroads of Eighth and Christian Streets were worse. These two dangerous intersections were at opposite ends of the street regularly called by the news media, "Dope Row" but was actually where Our Lady of Good Counsel Church, school, convent and rectory stood among the unusually high number of killings, narcotics sales and corpses lying with the trash in the gutters.[31]

Suburban living agreed with Sabella and his family. His wife was close to her relatives, so help with the children was available. Family members said that Philadelphia's Mafia boss welcomed the respite from the city's congestion, the cops on the take and gangsters' grievances. Salvatore and Maria owned a corner house with grass on all four sides, a spacious home, with pleasant memories to be had here. The Sabellas were becoming more americanized in their new neighborhood, learning to speak English more and less Sicilian. Their Anglo-Saxon Protestant neighbors were refreshing and never insensitive. The Sabellas would never live in the city again.

Salvatore Sabella was still accumulating more mileage with additional bootlegging associates now in the Philadelphia suburbs as well as in the city, south Jersey and in any other place where sales could be made.[32] His skills in organization, used for his personal, illegal and legal activities brought him in contact with many who were impressed with his seemingly endless energy.

Sabella's real power in Philadelphia however, was not to be underestimated despite that he never was a target for the press as other underworld favorites were. His influence was especially extensive during Prohibition, but quietly and in closed circles. Then, suddenly in 1927, Sabella the Mafioso, the leader of Philadelphia's Mafia Family, became a public figure. On a day celebrated as "Decoration Day" before Memorial Day in 1927, the Philadelphia Mafia would make history because the men who would figure prominently in the city's underworld for the next forty years were present in this incident.[33] A composite of the incident thus follows.[34]

John Scopoletti, a known gangster, was slowly driving west on Christian Street and passed by three Sicilian Friends standing at the intersection of Eighth and Christian Streets. Two of the Sicilians then approached a gang leader named, Anthony "Musky" Zanghi on both sides. One Sicilian gave Zanghi the "Judas greeting," i.e., a kiss on the cheek, while another smiled, laughed at the kiss and gave a hand signal to the approaching vehicle on Eighth Street. North of Christian, on Eighth Street, Joseph Zanghi, the nineteen year old brother of Anthony, and Vincent "Scabby" Cocozza came out of a restaurant and walked south parallel to the moving auto and towards the intersection where the three Sicilians lingered with Musky. Meanwhile, from the north, on Eighth, Scopoletti's car slowly approached the intersection. When the shot guns appeared at the windows, the Sicilian Friends drew their revolvers and all simultaneously fired at the two Zanghis and Cocozza.

In just seconds, the smoke cleared and the perforated bodies of Joseph Zanghi and Scabby were found dead in the street. A six year old Mario Lanza, then known as Freddie Cocozza, would recall later as an adult the memory of his uncle Vincent lying lifeless and on the blood-coated ground. His father would be called as a witness for the Commonwealth. Brain matter discharged from the shattered skulls and into the crevices of the street paving blocks. Unlike what the Pennsylvania Crime Commission reports wrote, no one else was wounded or injured.

HOW TWO MEN WERE SLAIN IN GANGSTERS' FEUD

The photo-diagram shows how Joseph Zanghi, nineteen, and Vincent Cocozza, thirty, were killed on 8th St. near Christian when an attack was made with pistols and shotguns by men in a moving automobile and other men on the street. "Musky" Zanghi, brother of Joseph, who later identified the alleged attackers and caused their arrest, is shown at upper left. "Musky" leader of a rival gang was the target for the attack, but escaped injury. A window at 824 S. 8th St. which was broken by the gangsters bullets, is shown at lower left.

(*EVENING BULLETIN*)

A few spectators jotted down Scopoletti's vehicle's license plate numbers amidst the loud wailing and screams. Disappearing down Eighth Street went the car with the three Friends, Sabella, John Avena and A. Domenico Pollina balancing on the running boards. Meanwhile, Anthony "Musky" Zanghi, the real target, went about in a daze, disoriented at first, then hysterical. He knew that he was intended to die, not his brother—he had been warned for weeks. Frenzied, the word uttered from Zanghi's mouth was, "Sabella.'

When the police arrived, Musky Zanghi admitted that he was the one who was supposed to be killed—the deceased were innocent victims, he said. Musky then resolved to give more unsolicited information to anyone who listened. Within seconds, the law and news media arrived and pressed close to Zanghi who was ready for anyone's question.

The next morning, Philadelphia's five leading newspapers ran headlines: "The Underworld's First Squealer!" It was unbelievable. It was such an unexpected turn of events that any news on Zanghi diverted the public's attention from Colonel Charles A. Lindbergh's epic transatlantic flight. "Unheard of!" The newspaper boys bellowed in pitching their papers. Dying gangsters would never violate this code of the underworld, even in their last moments of life, by telling who shot them. But here was Zanghi, called by newspapers, "Philadelphia's First Underworld Rat," who was prepared to bring down police, politicians and other gangsters at the height of Prohibition.

But sadly, gangland murders were so commonplace in the 1920s in Philadelphia that Joey Zanghi's and Scabby's deaths were regarded as just incidentals. In a society resigned to lawlessness, these casualties remained as names without personalities. Only funeral Masses at Our Lady of Good Counsel eulogized these gangsters as humans with souls.

Musky was nowhere near his grieving mother's side as she mourned her dead teenage son. The police thought it best to place "The Squealer" in protective custody while he rambled on what he knew about the double murders. Meanwhile, detectives had found Sabella and some of the others, eating and drinking at the home of Friend, Philip Pollina on the night of the shooting in what police interpreted as a "celebration feast." The *rapprisentanti* and his soldiers were then arrested and brought to City Hall for identification by Zanghi. No remarks about blood stains on their suits were noted.

Photographs show Sabella in his straw hat standing in a group with the others, some "made" Mafiosi, others of Italian ancestry not yet allowed as members into the Organization. These associates would later become mem-

Held in Connection With Street Murders

End of Gang Wa;
Predicted by P

Police photographs of alleged murderers from May 31, 1927 incident.
(*AS REPRINTED IN PUBLIC LEDGER*)

bers. Sabella was there, standing erect, chin up, as if in defiance to the camera who dared to capture his image. Moments later, John Avena and his neighbor, John Scopoletti were brought in, identified by Zanghi and joined the rest of the crew. The mug shots show all of the men as well-dressed, looking too unlikely to have been involved in a open-air gunfight on a busy Philadelphia street.

More than two weeks after the murders, on June 15, 1927, Acting Captain Kerns of the Sixth District Police arrested two more Friends, Andrea Restucci and Mike Macaluso, hoping that they would be witnesses for the Commonwealth Court. Musky had suggested that Kerns speak with them, not knowing of their relationship with Sabella. The two Mafiosi requested an interpreter who had just two statements from their mouths to translate: "What you think?" and "What should I do?" which was what Musky asked of these men and how they responded to him. After several minutes of a frustrating dialogue, Kerns then discharged them.

Had Musky not squealed on Sabella, we may not know about the Sicilian American Mafia in Philadelphia at this time, although the Organization and its members were not identified by law enforcement until decades later. Evidently the Mafia in Philadelphia had little control of the press, unlike with the police, prosecutors and politicians who produced as little paperwork on the incident as possible. (Refer to Appendix III.) The news media, whose accounts were more substantial than the legal documentation filed, was able to record several issues that concerned the local Mafia's character and activities during this state of its growth here.

First, the local newspapers in 1927 quoted Zanghi as saying that Sabella had sent for him weeks before the murders and said, "These boys have gone too far...this has got to stop. They are going to be taken." Collectively, the newspapers wrote that Zanghi said that he went to see Sabella at the "gin mills" where Sabella worked and asked him for a loan of money. Actually, admitted Zanghi, he wanted more money on top of that which he had already owed to Sabella. The *rapprisentanti* told Zanghi that he had lent him enough money and refused him more. But during the course of the dialogue, Sabella admonished little Zanghi to stop his gang from shaking-down the places that the Mafia was paid to protect. Word had reached Sabella that Zanghi continued to shoot up stores in "Little Italy" and to make threats. In keeping his obligation to his clientele, Sabella

60

HELD IN GANG WAR

Another police photograph of the seven accused from the May 31, 1927 incident. Note the misspelled names of Scopoletti, Pollina, Testa and Quaranta. This montage was put together in haste—Joe Ida was disqualified by Zanghi the same night.

Seven of the men arrested in connection with the killing of two men in a gangsters' feud on S. 8th St. They are: John Scapellitti, upper left; Salvatore Sabella, upper right; Joseph Ida, left centre; Paulo Domenico, right centre: John Avena, lower left: Dominick Testa, lower centre, and Luigi Quarenta, lower right.

warned Zanghi more than once to stay away. Zanghi kept refusing.[35]

In his defiance, Zanghi made Sabella look badly.

It was this arrogance by Zanghi that made the Mafia boss react.

The 1927 example serves well to explain a centuries-long Mafia practice. The protection rackets were another traditional activity that Mafiosi brought to the United States from western Sicily. The customers, or clients were asked, or asked by themselves, for protection by the Mafia for a price. In return, the Mafia staved off any shakedown artists or extortionists. It was a simple, reciprocal relationship bound by a fee, although there has been contrasting information on this form of Mafia income. As early as 1876, Leopoldo Franchetti witnessed paid protection in Sicily and documented that the Mafiosi protectors assumed the multiple roles of "capitalist" "entrepreneur" and "general manager."[36] Anton Blok reported that in western Sicily a practice of compensating the guardian of an estate was akin more to a tax.[37] Pino Arlacchi was in agreement with Blok in 1983 and placed the activity among the "predatory incomes" which sometimes used force.[38] According to one of Sabella's soldiers though, this was not the case in Philadelphia. It was more like what Diego Gambetta described as the private protection system of western Sicily's agrarian areas made into an "industry" in the modern urban world of Mafiosi.[39] Gambetta's understanding of the Mafia's paid protection business as a "commodity" is more in line to what Salvatore Sabella and his contemporaries practiced as a service business in which the customer/client was the valued commodity. There was no fee, if no protection. Sabella's clients' complaints, therefore, may have caused more than embarrassment—Sabella may have had to return money. Or worse yet, his reputation as a paid protector may have been sullied.

But there was another issue here. How else was Sabella to make Zanghi, whose ancestry was from eastern Sicily, learn respect?

Henner Hess rationalized the type of action taken by Sabella that resulted in the double murders. Hess called an act such as Sabella's, the "ultima ratio for the Mafioso, a sacrifice which he makes for the benefit of the public weal."[40] Giuseppe Montalbano, as referenced in Hess' work, stated a "Mafia rule" that mandated "to help one another to revenge in blood any affront suffered."[41] These, along with this Sicilian proverb, explained Sabella's reason to sanction such an incident:

"*A cu ti leva lu pani levacci la vita.*"
(If someone takes away your bread, take his life.)

Sabella did, in effect, use extreme violence to enforce Mafia norms upon the "Little Italy" community whose culture equated fear with honor and respect.

When those Friends and associates identified by Musky were brought in to City Hall on May 30, 1927, the Mafiosi looked at Zanghi and ridiculed his lack of composure in front of the police and detectives. Zanghi was shaken, but still talkative. This was the same Zanghi whom the papers called, "the diminutive one." He had a gold front tooth. He was just a bit over five feet tall. When the Mafiosi and their associates laughed at him, an enraged Zanghi threw a punch at Sabella that knocked him onto the floor. There then was a sudden silence. Then all eyes turned to Sabella as he arose from the floor. The *rapprisentanti*, described by the newspapers as the "biggest of the lot" whom Zanghi had called a "dirty dog," the "filthy dirty dog who shot Joey" in the forehead with the fatal bullet was felled in one punch.[42]

This was not the first time that Zanghi tested Sabella's patience. Besides Zanghi's testimony of "Sabella did this," the boss was to figure in Zanghi's statement numerous times.

Accordingly, Sabella and his Friends made the first move and did what law enforcement was unable to do: close Zanghi's mouth with a pay-off. This action was usually effective—the Sicilian Mafiosi paid Zanghi reputedly between "$25,000.00 to $50,000.00" to begin a new life far from the city.[43] Zanghi took the money and temporarily left Philadelphia, but his eleven page notarized statement to the detectives' stenographer stayed with the Court and unknowingly threatened not just the city's underworld but its criminal justice system as well. In addition to this, the news media duly kept atop every detail of this unprece- dented case with Zanghi vowing to avenge his brother's murder with the "tell-all" on bootlegging, gambling, prosti- tution, graft, bribery and murder— and, how local law enforcement allowed these crimes to continue.

The newspapers wrote that Zanghi identified all of the men involved at the murder scene and their illegal activi- ties which would seemingly have sealed their fates to life sentences or death, if one believed Zanghi. He did have some credibility problems, however. Newspapers did not hesitate to elaborate on Zanghi's criminal record and how he was able to be an "insider" to the underworld's wide range of interests. In 1919, Zanghi was found guilty of the first degree murder of Police Officer Joseph Swiercynski. The homicide record read of a "...colored man that was held up by two men [who]...went into the saloon at 9th and Christian. Swiercynski went into saloon and said he'd lock up [the] first man that came out. Zanghi came out and shot him [the policeman]."[44] On appeal, Zanghi produced an alibi witness who freed him from the ultimate penalty at Eastern State Penitentiary. But this was not the end of his record. Musky was a convicted highjacker, married two women at the same time and had questionable relation-

64

ships with some loose women and a "male exotic dancer" who testified for him and against the Mafiosi.[45]

Zanghi never said, probably because he did not know, that Sabella was the leader of a very powerful group. Most thought that John Scopoletti was this gang's boss. What Zanghi did say was that his gang of about five was insignificant compared to the "one hundred!" who opposed him and wanted him dead. Sabella was part of this gang, he said and this "gang" came down from outside of Pennsylvania to do "business" here. Of course, Musky knew that on the evening of the murders, the police and detectives had arrested at Pollina's house four men from New Brunswick, New Jersey, the back-up crew for Sabella who also were involved in underworld operations.[46]

The information on Philadelphia's Mafia at this time indicates how far the Organization was progressing: that the Mafia in Philadelphia, as in other cities nationwide, was using non-Sicilians as "associates" to do free-lance work; that interstate associations continued and were strong; and that there were more contacts with those of mainland Italian ancestry in business, not the more traditional *paesano* or Friend. The network of contacts was thus broadened with the intention of furthering more income.

These double murders spread the share of embarrassment beyond Sabella and the local Philadelphia Mafia—the Philadelphia Police now had to explain their relationship with the Mafia. Cautious as they were to go through the regular process of an arrest, the city's police guarded the handling of these particular murders. So inordinate and substantial was the amount of collusion among the Mafia, police and District Attorney's Office, that after the news media covered the first part of the trial, there never was more publicity in the subsequent trials, possibly because the prosecutor acted with great reluctance to proceed.

65

A. Domenico Pollina, born in Caccamo, Sicily, arrived in the U.S. around 1924, when Mussolini's arrests of Mafiosi in Sicily began. He joined his brother and Sabella's Family upon arrival.

(U.S. DEPT OF JUSTICE, ORGANIZED CRIME STRIKE FORCE & FEDERAL BUREAU OF INVESTIGATION)

Antonio Domenico Pollina in 1927.
(1892—1993)

Of the seven men arrested for the double murders, the two associates of Italian ancestry (Dominic Festa and John Scopoletti), and the three Sicilian Friends, (Sabella, Avena and Pollina) were finally released after a few weeks in jail and some calm with the press. Prominent businessmen in South Philadelphia paid for the Friends' bails after raising money.[47] Joseph Ida, arrested and taken to City Hall with the others, was disqualified by Zanghi as part of the murder group and released. But Luigi "Lou" Quaranta, a young Mafioso from Sicily was held over because he rode in Scopoletti's car with Festa.

One learns how the Mafia and other gangsters of the 1920s understood society, the legal system and human nature by this incident. "Someone had to take the responsibility for Joey Zanghi's and Cocozza's death," one of

Sabella's Friends said. Why? "It had to be someone," but not everyone involved. One person was enough. Society would not have wanted anything more, although witnesses and forensics proved otherwise. Luigi Quaranta, who would serve almost eight years at Eastern State Penitentiary before his sentence was commuted, became the scapegoat for all in taking "the rap" with not just one, but two guilty verdicts. The all-male jury however, recommended "life imprisonment" for him instead of the death penalty, the only defendant to testify that he was neither a bootlegger nor involved in any illegal activity.

John Avena, whom the Court originally named as the first defendant to be tried, was moved to a different position by the Commonwealth Court. The priority of the other defendants was also changed so that Sabella would be the last to testify at Quaranta's trial. Sabella would provide four witnesses to vouch that he was not at the place at the time of the murders.[48] The *rapprisentanti* took the stand and said simply and tersely that he was married, had several children and lived outside of the city. As for an occupation, Sabella admitted that he was indeed a bootlegger, owned an oil and cheese store and ran a café at Eighth and Catharine Streets for a man nicknamed, "New York Mike." He added that he also owned a candy store at Eighth and Morris Streets and that "Michael Maggio was his godfather."[49] It is not known why it was necessary for Sabella to mention Maggio's name. His testimony nonetheless was unchallenged by the prosecution. No difficult questions, no indictable questions. Nothing he said would have indicated that he was anyone special, even in the underworld.

Sabella admitted that he knew Zanghi, but denied having lent him money or that Zanghi had asked him for money. The boss further denied any other contact with Zanghi, especially in the May 30th incident. Sabella was still detained in a local prison; but as soon as bail was set and Quaranta was sentenced, the *rapprisentanti* went back to whatever work awaited him.

Bail was set at $10,000.00 each for Sabella, Avena and Pollina, Friends apart from the next two defendants, the associates, Festa and Scopoletti, who would be tried in Court by the fall of 1927. Zanghi's statement had been inadmissible to Court and he never returned to testify in the latter's trials. It did not matter. Festa and Scopoletti were found, "not guilty" by October of that year. But Sabella, Avena and Pollina had their trials for two counts of first degree murder continued to 1933, by consent of the Philadelphia District Attorney's Office.[50]

The Pennsylvania Crime Commission reports document that Sabella was deported after this 1927 arrest, but this was not true. The boss' illegal immigration status was not discovered at this time. Moreover, he was the father of six U.S.-born children by this time and unlikely deportable. But more importantly, Sabella was somewhat protected by Philadelphia's law enforcement and local prosecutors who did not seem to care to discuss Sabella with Federal authorities. Real estate records from 1928 also attest to a very busy Sabella who was involved in a number of transactions in the Pennsylvania and New Jersey suburbs. Circumstances and events around Sabella went on as if his detention had not occurred.

What Zanghi had caused was now set aside for business to continue. But the public exposure had a negative impact on Sabella. The Zanghi-Cocozza murders may have portrayed Sabella now more in the view as a "gangster" with blood on his hands rather than just a "bootlegger." In the past, Sabella had escaped many criminal incidents in which he was directly involved, and which managed to keep his name out of the press. The 1927 murders, however, portrayed him, the other Friends and associates as threats to

68

the community's welfare, just by allowing neighborhood residents to witness the violence.

Prior violent incidents involving Sabella were more discreet. For example, the first public incident that would have had a far-reaching impact on Philadelphia's Mafia while Sabella was boss may have been the murder of Leo Lanzetti because his death, unknown to most, was ordered by Sabella.[51]

• • • • • • • •

Other Gangsters and Conflicts in "Little Italy"
● ●

The Lanzetti brothers began their criminal careers
during Sabella's administration of the local Family and
would prove to be one of the many gangs to antagonize the
Friends. The Lanzettis' approximate twenty years of criminal stardom began in their youth, by the early 1920s.[52] As
local celebrities, they were known throughout Center City,
North, West and South Philadelphia, but more in "Little
Italy" where they were born and raised. Neapolitan in
ancestry, the six brothers came from what the neighbors
described as "religious parents...such nice people who did-
n't deserve kids like them." Their father tried desperately
to eke out a living in one of the first Italian restaurants in
Philadelphia. He tried to manage a hotel named after
President William H. Taft. Somehow the poverty of their
youth never left the older Lanzetti brothers' memories.

The news media lavished undue space, almost daily, to
the Lanzettis. Leo, Pius (sometimes called "Harry"),
William (or Hugo), Teo (short for Teodoro), Ignatius (sometimes called Sylvester) and Lucien had annoyed
Philadelphia's Mafia as well as the local police as each

entered adolescence. They were involved in every vice and crime of the day for about twenty years, ending in the late 1930s. For about a decade, law enforcement begged the brothers to leave Philadelphia to commit crime elsewhere. As a bit of irony, the press began to claim that the brothers were named after popes. By the early 1930s, at least one reporter dubbed them, "The First Family of Crime" in Philadelphia.[53] It was not until 1939, when a body found in a burlap bag in a suburban Main Line town was identified as Willie Lanzetti, that the remaining brothers left Philadelphia permanently with their mother.

The Lanzetti brothers' gang was not too large, but they were the most popular gang in Philadelphia during Prohibition, thanks to the news media who considered them good copy. The brothers' reputations were based mostly on their ability to beat the rap on the hundreds of arrests that they amassed. Reporters loved to document the frustration of police officials like Inspector John Driscoll, who groaned, "We have picked up the Lanzettis one hundred times!"[54] The gangsters would get arrested while others would have precluded the arrest process with a fast pay-off. Conscious of the press' watchful eyes, the brothers used the news media for what it could do for them in their criminal activities. The reporters would read the police's blotter with any Lanzetti arrest, write about it, then publicize the following day that, "The Lanzettis Beat The Rap Again!"[55]

Cavalier attitudes aside, the Lanzettis often had quotable retorts for the law: "Lock me up, I gotta prove I ain't no doper," Teo Lanzetti once told Sergeant William Leinhouser of the Philadelphia Narcotics Squad. Another brother openly threatened in Court "to blow off" the head of Assistant District Attorney Vincent Carroll if his brother Lucien "gets five years. It's a frameup..." Judge MacNeille, defending the District Attorney's Office, told three of the brothers present at the proceeding, "You have no courage, you're just bold" before citing them with contempt.[56] While the Lanzettis' smart-aleck answers and wise cracks were often printed, their manipulative ways to commit crime spoke louder. "When the Lanzettis get low on cash, and the players are striking the numbers a bit too regularly, one of the Lanzetti gang is instructed to tip off Police to the existence of a bank...The Lanzettis don't pay off! I've said so again and again. They're welchers!" said Inspector Driscoll.[57] Though the private cries in the neighborhood too often went without recourse, they were nonetheless louder than Driscoll's comments.

Some of the Lanzetti brothers did put in some brief times in jail, but even there they would get the media's ear and pen in hand. Such as the time when in 1924 Willie, Pius and Ignatius were sent to Holmesburg Prison together

LEO LANZETTI
Born 1893 — Died at age 32

Leo Lanzetti's arrest record:

March 20, 1918 arrested as an inmate of a gambling house.

December 17, 1921 arrested as an inmate of gambling house.

May 9, 1923 arrested for suspicion of possession of narcotics.

May 29, 1923 arrested as a suspected narcotic addict.

December 25, 1923 arrested on charge of selling narcotics.

August 22, 1925 "Rubbed out" by five masked men.

(SOURCE: *RECORD*)

on narcotics offenses. Bored with trying to amuse themselves inside, the brothers staged a hunger strike and contended that the prison food was inedible. Judge Harry S. McDevitt, the "Hanging Judge" and one of the city's most powerful leaders in the 1920s then assembled a grand jury, fearing a riot and the brothers' growing number of sympathizers. The jurors found that the food was "good"—the brothers only wanted the attention.[58]

Lives of crime began early for the Lanzetti brothers. They thieved and were arrested repeatedly for the crimes of "disorderly person," "suspicious character" and "loitering." Beat cops occasionally took pride in slapping the brothers around, just to remind them of who was in charge. Captain Jimmy Ryan reputedly used to smack Pius in the face and Pius took it without disrespect. The Lanzettis sold and used illegal drugs such as morphine, opium and marijuana. Sometimes for their own protection, they would walk into police stations and ask the public's guardians to place them in jail cells for their own safety against other gangsters.[59] No one in the Lanzettis' old neighborhood ever considered them as "just good boys turned bad" or "folk heroes" or anything forgiving. On the contrary, the Lanzettis were never known to share their spoils with the needy, to give to any type of legitimate charity or to help anyone but themselves. It was this selfish quality that left an impression on everyone who knew them. Women were not drawn to their dark good looks because they were afraid of the danger surrounding the gangsters. Others in the underworld rolled their eyes and shook their heads when the Lanzettis made the papers. At best, they were considered common criminals.

The news media may have fed the Lanzettis with the confidence they dearly appreciated, because, to the Mafia, the Lanzettis were just another small local gang. The opinion was apparently mutual. Sabella must have had the last of his patience spent on the Lanzettis by the summer of 1925. The boss was said to be reluctant to spill blood, but he knew that the Lanzettis cost either him, his Family or his clients considerable harm. Leo Lanzetti was the oldest brother whom the Mafia used as an example. "He didn't give the Mafia any respect," said one familiar with the circumstances around Leo's untimely death in August of 1925. Giving respect to a Sicilian Mafioso could mean many things—Leo's tragic type of death indicated what he might have done to raise the ire of Sabella. "Make me look good, Tony. This will be the last time," Leo was said to have told his barber at Seventh and Bainbridge Streets. As Leo walked out of the shop, a car with a New York license plate drove "...four young men...all wearing masks" who began to shoot at him.[60] The police homicide report wrote that when taken to Pennsylvania Hospital, Leo had "...gun shots: two in head, one in thigh, one in face and one in chest."

"Unsolved" was noted in the file.[61]

No one knew if the Lanzetti brothers ever understood what the Sicilian American Mafia in Philadelphia was, because they continued to be a nuisance to the Organization as well as to the Jewish Mob and other gangs. The brothers were criminally incompatible with these gangs, especially with the Sicilians who still were characteristically foreign and certainly more conservative in underworld affairs. The case of Joseph Bruno, however, lends much to speculation on whether the local Family had members who may have been more progressive than their leader and traditional Mafia norms.

After Leo Lanzetti was killed, the Philadelphia Police tied his death to that of a young gangster named Joseph Bruno. A dope pusher, Bruno, born Joseph LoCascio in Brooklyn, New York, was shot multiple times on the north-east corner of Eighth and Christian Streets just a few days before Leo. Bruno was said to have originally been a plasterer by trade, but came to Philadelphia to sell narcotics by about 1918. He apparently had his own gang, clubhouse and supplier coming from his native New York in 1925. In the summer of that year, Bruno was shot twelve times with .45 calibre bullets on his right side, his left side full of buckshot and yet, for two days in agony, he refused to tell who shot him. The press wrote that Bruno was killed because he welched on the middleman who brought him morphine and cocaine.[62] Lieutenant Peter Sheller of Philadelphia's "Murder Squad" had asked the dying Bruno to disclose his killer's identity, but he declined. The police, however, should have been able to collar their killer. One officer witnessed the killing, testified, but still did not change the mind of the prosecutor who wrote, "Nolle pros" for the charges against Ignatius Lanzetti. "Lack of evidence" was the official reason.[63]

The day after Bruno died, a "pistol battle between gangsters at Ninth and Christian" broke out with gun shots exchanged from the rowhouses' rooftops and automobiles racing past the pushcarts.[64] Again, two days later, another young gangster was shot, but only wounded, at Eighth and Christian Streets, and no one was apprehended. "Unsolved" appears in the police's homicide records most often at this time with the flurry of gangland murders from the scores of mobsters confounding law enforcement. Decomposed bodies found in the marshes where the Schuylkill and Delaware Rivers meet were not uncommon. Police attributed some mysterious deaths to "dope peddling," "bootlegging" of course, and even to rows over women. Crime, at times, was more acceptable because it was not beatable.

"Italian" crime in Philadelphia though, was experiencing some broad developments during Sabella's tenure in the 1920s. Although there were distractions by other gangs, the Mafia, though not clearly recognized, was indeed noticed by local police who were also able to distinguish the Sicilians from the Neapolitan Black Handers based on each group's activities, interactions, structure and relationships within the community. Philadelphia's Finest did not have to know about the hundreds of miles separating the region of Campania from western Sicily to know that the two vastly different cultures produced two ideologically diverse deviant groups. During Sabella's time as Philadelphia's Mafia boss, the differences between the Mafia and Black Hand in the city were very clear, especially to those victims who made reports to the police. By 1926, the last recorded murders in Philadelphia involving the Black Hand signified the end of this underdeveloped criminal entity.[65] An absence of strong leadership was only one reason why this group was fated for short-term existence.

Another dimension to Sabella's Family, though unsupporting "Italian" crime was the acceptance of Sicilian Mafiosi who were fleeing Benito Mussolini's arrests. Arriving with letters from their Sicilian bosses, these men joined Sabella's Family, were unsuspected of any illegal activities, and, therefore, had no arrest records to indicate their presence at that time in Sabella's group.

In terms of analyzing Salvatore Sabella's role as *rapprisentanti* and how he operated the local Family, his work was largely unnoticed. Likewise, his criminal mishaps were quickly masked. One soldier characterized him as "fair" while another said that Sabella was a "good man," in respect to the dead boss. Sabella's responsibilities were far from light, impersonal, or limiting. He oversaw Philadelphia's and South Jersey's Mafia-influenced operations and was expected to initiate income-producing activities to justify the Family's place within the national Organization.

76

Sabella's men were also expected to reflect the Family's *raison d'être* in various businesses, legitimate or illicit. One of Sabella's men described the alcohol industry locally as one that began at a simple still. Molasses was used in lieu of sugar to produce a liquor with a proof that could top to 200%. Flavors were added and water "cut" the proof down to more tolerable, potable drinks. Transporting the alcohol product was often more dangerous than others because highjacking was just as feared as fires at stills. No need to feel police pressure, however: arrests for bootlegging were curtailed by paying the regular beat cop $2.00 a week in advance. Alcohol, as a commodity in a system, became the base for the local Mafia's income and power, more than any other illegal activity during this time.

Parallel examples of corrupt law enforcement and politics link the Philadelphia Mafia to other Mafia Families' rise in power in other major cities during Prohibition because the local civil servants purposely expressed a lack of interest in enforcing Federal law. Nelli wrote that violating the "Volstead Act was more acceptable to the public as well as 'cleaner' than prostitution or the narcotic traffic."[66] Pitkin saw this period as "when a great part of the American public, otherwise more or less law-abiding, defied the drastic antiliquor laws and when bootleggers became more heroes than criminals in their eyes."[67] Johnson's take on the politicians' "major role" in Prohibition was by way of the lists of casualties resulting from a relaxed law enforcement: over four hundred gangsters died in Chicago in the bootlegging conflicts before Prohibition's repeal. "That was not typical, however," wrote Johnson.[68] From about 1925 to the end of 1928, approximately twenty-two bootlegging-related murders occurred in Philadelphia, mostly in South Philadelphia and sometimes within the proximity of law enforcement who often found that underworld affairs were best left to be resolved within that realm.

South Philadelphia's history of politics and crime had been formed well before those from the Mediterranean settled here. Back in the 1840s, the Irish Catholics who fled a famine-ravished Ireland to live in the first rowhouses in Moyamensing Township, today's South Philadelphia, connected politics to crime in many public incidents that ranged from voting to arson.[69] Sabella, like those before him, only continued a Philadelphia custom of paying to fix, pay-offs and collusion to the Republican Party which he supported as did his Friends.

The South Philadelphia venue of Sabella's tenure was not unlike its nineteenth century character with many residents who had flexible deviant tendencies and inflexible attitudes towards mainstream Philadelphia society. Culturally alienated from those who lived and worked in the Philadelphia of William Penn's plan, the dwellers of South Philadelphia from the mid-nineteenth century had much in common with those in the next century. Some residents had believed that the geographic location of "Little Italy" led to the brush of economic prejudice from city government because the majority were of the lower class and had peculiar characteristics. The quaint lifestyles of some were often near squalor and filth. Visually distracted from some impressionable visits, most Center City politicians distanced themselves from this area of Philadelphia, leaving this neighborhood to develop its own autonomous government somewhat independent from the rest of the city. Sam Bass Warner connected the ecological with the psychological: "Isolation bred parochialism and the shelter of insulated ghettoes."[70]

But while no law enforcement could claim complete control over this area of Philadelphia, neither did any one criminal enterprise, organized or not. Gangs such as the long-running Irish Catholic "Killers" were prominent in South Philadelphia before and after the Civil War, as were the "Gumballs" and "Snakes," until other ethnic groups arrived to claim their territories for criminal activity.[71] Every vice would be cultivated in this section of South Philadelphia, and local politicians too often would encourage the tradition of criminality through participation. In time, South Philadelphia's individual identity became synonymous with corruption and violence.

Criminal gangs of simple organization, with a leader and some members characterized the Irish Catholic, British Protestant, Eastern European Jewish and African American groups. The more complex "gang," the Sicilian Mafia with its titled hierarchy, had not just its own unusual characteristics, but preferences when it came to unlawful activities. Each organized crime gangs' involvements with the various criminal interests ran in degrees, with some groups eschewing certain types of crimes that may have cultural biases. Such was the case with illegal narcotics in Sabella's Mafia in the 1920s. "Little Italy's" Eighth and Christian Streets' intersection had become the reputed "Dope Curb Market" in South Philadelphia, at least as it was documented in the First National Narcotics Convention in 1926. Held in Washington, D.C., the literature that highlighted Philadelphia's drug problem referenced only two sites in the entire city where easy purchases of any narcotic could be made: at Eighth and Vine Streets, and at Eighth and Christian Streets where "Dope Row" ran westward to Ninth Street to include Our Lady of Good Counsel Church, rectory, convent and school. No spokesperson from Philadelphia at this conference, however, was able to provide information as to which gang was responsible for the sales of narcotics there.[72]

It is unclear whether drugs were an interest of the Mafia during Prohibition. But the evidence indicates that Mafiosi in Philadelphia in the 1920s strongly considered narcotics as a commodity worth undertaking. In Mafia phi-

79

23 Policemen, Under Arrest, on March to Cells

Charged with accepting graft from bootleggers, Captain Charles Cohen, eight sergeants, three detectives and eleven patrolmen were arrested on orders of District Attorney Monaghan late last night. The men in citizen's clothes, shielding his face, is Captain Cohen. Beyond him, bareheaded, is Assistant Superintendent of Police James J. Hearne, who stripped the twenty-three badges and suspended them when they reached the city hall cellroom.

(PUBLIC LEDGER)

losophy, it was traditionally understood that narcotics, sex crimes, counterfeiting and kidnapping were abominable. Junkies disgusted the community and befuddled the legal and medical professionals who had not a clue on whether to criminalize the habit or to medically treat an offender of the law.

Alcohol, on the other hand, never raised any doubts. And the Mafia nationally knew that Prohibition was a matter of politics, pushed by temperance activists and those who wanted to control immigrants' behaviors.[73] The extremely low rate of arrests for the alcohol violators in South Philadelphia's "Little Italy" neighborhood confirms the city's tolerance for alcohol and those who were making it in vast quantities.[74] What is notable about the Philadelphia Mafia Family's alcohol business is that under Sabella, there were no newsworthy "bootlegging battles" that resulted in deaths. Nor were there any conflicts with the Jewish or native-born mobsters who were cited by the local grand jury as the gangs who "dominated the liquor trade in the city"—Max "Boo Boo" Hoff and Mickey Duffy, né Cusick.[75] Sabella's Friends and associates apparently were successful not only in staving off violent competitors but also in forging relationships with the major bootlegging factions so as not to appear threatening, but trusting.

With regard to gambling as a Mafia money interest, there were no indications that Sabella's Mafia was competing with the Lanzetti brothers' gang or any other group, such as the Jewish Mob before 1930. The information from the 1927 Zanghi-Cocozza murder trials does not mention gambling as a major Mafia activity at that time, but again, members who were acting independently may have begun some bookmaking without Sabella's participation and control.

• • • • • • • • •

Ever-Evading the Public Eye
● ●

A year had passed since Sabella, Avena and Pollina had been arrested. Local newspapers connected Friend Luigi Quaranta's denied appeal in June of 1928 to an explosion of gunfire at Eleventh and Locust Streets in Center City Philadelphia by men riding in an auto with New Jersey license plates.[76] But the double murders in 1927 supposedly caused law enforcement to remain alert to more unsolved murders in the interim. Musky Zanghi, after all, was still living somewhere in or near Philadelphia and obviously still had revenge on his mind with relation to Sabella and the Friends. In July of 1928, a car driving west on Christian Street stopped just after passing Passyunk Avenue and eyed the flour salesman talking in front of his office. "Hey, Catania!" yelled one of the riders. George Catania, a Friend from Upper Darby, approached the vehicle at the same time that two automatic machine guns and two revolvers appeared to fire upon him. Making a graceful turn, Catania fell to a total of fifteen bullets that pierced through his body. The sloppy gunsmen wounded three others, including a female and a young boy before driving

82

away. Captain Kerns and his policemen had heard the forty or more rounds spray the rowhouses and by-standers but, as he told the press, "nobody knows anything and nobody saw anything."[77]

Violence continued to reverberate throughout the City of Philadelphia after the Zanghi-Cocozza murders but whatever Sabella did to counter Zanghi's persistent revenge was known only to the Friends. Sabella may indeed have had this situation with the errant Zanghi under control, but it was not public knowledge. And it is doubtful that local law enforcement would have been involved in Sabella's matter unless Sabella asked. This was nothing new to the Mafia. Nick Gentile recounted numerous instances in New York when Mafiosi cooperated with the police to maintain public order or requested law enforcement's cooperation where only underworld figures would be harmed.[78] Gentile added that one New York City police captain threatened to publicly expose Mafia activities if "innocent civilians" became victimized.[79] Slowly, corruption within the city's criminal justice system began to be realized publicly, beginning in 1926 when the Philadelphia Law Associates published a Crimes Survey Committee Report which concluded that "a great many offenses are never prosecuted for which there may be several explanations...the offenses of...gambling and illicit liquor selling are the common practices of many persons who are not disturbed by criminal prosecutions. The explanation may be police corruption."[80] It was not until the end of 1928, that the criminal justice system of Philadelphia surfaced, prompted by the recent murders of the Philadelphia Athletics mascot, Hughey McLoon, and then, Dan O'Leary. The cumulative effect of these and previous killings on Philadelphia's neighborhoods revealed that underworld influence had an impact on every resident in the city. Led by the same judge who presided over Dominic Festa's and

Demands Clean-up

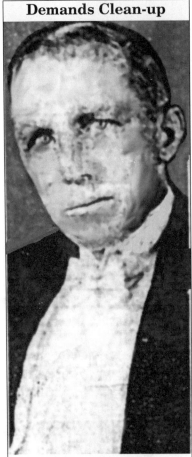

JUDGE EDWIN O. LEWIS
Born in Richmond, Va., July 12, 1879.
Came to Philadelphia in 1896, entered the University of Pennsylvania Law School and was graduated in 1902.
Took active part in independent political movements and was elected to Common Council in 1907.
Was independent candidate for Sheriff in 1911 and was defeated by A. Lincoln Acker.
Appointed Assistant City Solicitor in 1912.
In 1923, with the indorsement of the organization, he was selected to succeed Judge Norris S. Barratt as a member of Court of Common Pleas No. 2.

(*PUBLIC LEDGER*)

John Scopoletti's trials in the Zanghi-Cocozza murders, the esteemed Edwin O. Lewis,[81] and assisted by District Attorney John Monaghan a Grand Jury was convened to determine how close the city's police were with local bootleggers. The result was the dismissal of nearly one hundred police officers. Sam Griffin, the "Millionaire Cop" had bank deposits totalling almost $500,000.00, while other officers owned shore houses and large luxury automobiles. District Attorney Monaghan put the indicted policemen's bank books on display. They were the answers to Judge Lewis' question, "What happened to millions in graft collected (for) years?"[82] By the end of 1928, it was confirmed that Philadelphia's Police Department was rife with corruption, though the officers may have only been at the lowest level of the corruption organization. The Grand Jury, however, cited evidence that the policemen had been involved with Max "Boo Boo" Hoff, Max Hassel, Mickey Duffy and other gangsters. Neither Sabella's name,

84

nor that of any member of the local Mafia was ever mentioned.

Indeed, this corruption scandal became public one year after Sabella and the others arrested in the Zanghi-Cocozza murder trials had testified unhesitantly that yes, they were "bootleggers," even before Judge Lewis' Court. But the Friends were never arrested for alcohol offenses then, or after, in Philadelphia during the enforcement of the Volstead Act. And at no time did anyone ever question the special relationship between Sabella's Family and the Philadelphia Police or District Attorney's Office, although it is difficult to believe that Judge Lewis was not aware of the interactions.

Prohibition brought out more than corruption—it brought out the worst and the best in the bootleggers. By 1929, conflicts in most criminal groups, whether organized or not, caused enough alarm to prepare for some wide-spread bloodshed throughout the United States because of alcohol sales and distribution. The battles would not be ethnically-based. As Pitkin noted, "Whatever their ethnic origins, their members were known as 'gangsters,' 'racke-teers,' 'hoodlums' often as 'mobsters.' Ethnic labels disap-peared."[83] The same was true for Philadelphia's underworld, although those gangs of mainly Jewish, south-ern Italian and Sicilian ancestries had interstate ties with their respective groups that ran from Pennsylvania to New Jersey to New York, with the controls for every ethnicity arising from the latter's base. Representatives from these groups eventually were present in a type of conference in Atlantic City, New Jersey in 1929. But whatever was the result seemed to have no influence on what was transpiring among the Sicilian Americans in every Mafia Family in the country.

Prohibition's profits caused drastic changes in New York's Sicilian colonies and with the five Mafia Families there. With the accelerated growth in wealth from alcohol profits came faster acculturation to all things "American," often with unexpected results. Suddenly the lack of restraint was gone—the more conservative of the group believed that more of the wealth should be spread around to others. A situation arose when some Sicilian American Mafiosi in New York felt unjustifiably pressured by Giuseppe (Joseph) Masseria because he wanted some of their bootlegging profits as "tribute." He was called the *capo dei capi*, but there never officially was one by that title in Sicily.[84] Undisputedly, he had the most wealth of the five New York bosses and his power allowed him to weigh in with additional clout. Mafioso Nick Gentile recalled Masseria's strong, "direct relations with the police" in New York which solidified his position among other contenders in the liquor trade.[85]

His nickname was "the Boss" — "Joe the Boss," and he knew that was how he was referred to. By 1929 it was known that the most powerful boss in the United States was already engaging in warfare, mostly in New York City. Howard Abadinsky called Masseria a "Neapolitan" to fit into his theory of the "two major factions of Italian organized crime."[86] Stephen Fox placed Masseria from Sciacca.[87] If this was true, it would have caused some local conflict with the Norristown Sciaccatani and their neighboring Philadelphia Family members who were on the opposing side. But nothing happened in the city or suburbs because, as Gentile said, the Masseria that he knew personally was from Marsala in western Sicily.[88] Masseria rose to his position as *rapprisentanti* of his Family, one of the Five Families of New York, through his association with the Corleonese Morello Family, once powerful in Harlem, the Bronx and Brooklyn since the 1890s.[89] Masseria escaped a terrifying shooting in the early 1920s after he "made his bones" through his brawn, which impressed the Morellos.

They then took him in as one of their own. It was Joseph Bonanno's opinion that Masseria placed Peter "Clutch Hand" Morello as his underboss and let him run the Family in what seemed more like co-rule rather than by order of the representative.[90]

By 1929 it was a fact that Masseria was forcing the Castellammaresi of New York, Sabella's *paesani*, to pay him respect.

An interesting network was in place in 1929 though— Masseria was with the Corleonesi who were aligned with the Sciaccatani from lower Manhattan and Brooklyn, but the Philadelphia Mafia Family who sided with Salvatore Maranzano and the Castellammaresi in New York and who lived near the Sciaccatani in Montgomery County had no local interactions. One explanation may be that the suburban Mafiosi by that time were too old for war and had no younger generation of Mafiosi there because they did not pass the Mafia Tradition on to the U.S.-born sons.

In any event, the Castellammarese Wars provided the stuff of legends. In reality the internecine conflicts among the Mafia Families nationally from 1927 to the fall of 1931 signalled the end of the Sicilian American Mafia and beginning of a new, hybrid organization. The individuals who initiated the conflict were equally fictionalized except to Nick Gentile and Joseph Bonanno who lived through the "war" and had personal contacts with Joe the Boss and his rival, Salvatore Maranzano. Nick Gentile's views on "Massaria" differed from Bonanno's. Whereas the younger Bonanno, a Castellammarese, regarded Masseria darkly, Gentile expressed the opinion that it was Maranzano who continuously killed Masseria's men instead of trying to compromise. Then Maranzano, upon Masseria's death, gave himself the title, *"capo dei capi."* [91] When Bonanno hesitated to admit Maranzano's hubris, Gentile was direct: he recalled that Maranzano was a "Johnny-come-lately" to the

American underworld in the late 1920s and wanted the power, not the money, from Prohibition's gains.[92] Maranzano asserted himself by blood. And Philadelphia's Family's involvement began with Sabella's ties to Maranzano and the other Castellammaresi in New York.

These Castellammaresi in New York began to fight and to defend themselves in 1927.[93] That same year, perhaps after the killings commenced, Salvatore Sabella "opened the books" and held an initiation ceremony that counted among the new members, Harry Riccobene, not yet seventeen.[94] The teenage Mafioso represented an element within the local Family that was not unique to this city, but his independence did pose some challenges to Sabella. Harry was from a long line of Mafiosi in Enna, Sicily, and his

HARRY RICCOBENE.
Born in 1910.

(PHILADELPHIA POLICE)

father Mario had been in the Philadelphia Family longer than Sabella had been a member. Harry, though, had known Philadelphia's underworld from its lowest quarters and gained most of his experience on the street with the common criminals, unlike other Mafiosi. His birthright was in the Mafia, but Harry exhibited few of the traditional behaviors associated with other members. For example, in April of 1929, Harry got his first "pinch"—the charge was "Playfully pointing."[95] Instead of a pay-off to the magistrate or to the arresting officer, Harry spent the next six months in a jail cell. Not desiring any compromise with the civil servants as his fellow Mafiosi, Harry established himself then, as with every succeeding boss in Philadelphia, as someone who would not depend on his Family, possibly because no one in his age group compared to him in pedigree and in his criminal credentials. "I thieved with the Lanzettis," he said, and sold illegal narcotics, admittedly. But he was also Sabella's youngest soldier, and when taken to New York with Sabella, Harry would be the youngest Mafioso in the twenty-two months that he spent defending the Castellammaresi and their interests.[96]

Sabella spent his time in New York sporadically, as there was no evidence to determine any long stays there in either the "safe houses" or any place there where "laying down the mattresses" accommodated him. During 1928, he was involved in some real estate transactions in Pennsylvania and in New Jersey.[97] In 1929 Sabella, amidst the reports on skirmishes and casualties in New York, found an unwelcome surprise in May—Alfonse "Scarface" Capone, a Neapolitan who arrived in Philadelphia by way of the Chicago underworld.

Capone already had relationships with Sicilians in New York's boroughs, like Frankie Uale (Yale) and Joe Masseria, to whom he was said to send tribute money from Chicago. Evidently, Capone did know about Massseria's

"Alphonsus" Capone's Philadelphia criminal record of 1929.

(PHILADELPHIA POLICE)

plans with the various Sicilian colonies and Sicilian American Mafiosi Families in New York in order to make a decision on what his role might or might not be in the Sicilians' internecine war. What was fact was that Capone sided with Masseria.

Word from New York's Castellammarese colony reached Sabella rather quickly on how to handle Capone. Why Capone came to Philadelphia may have been part of his plan to show Masseria that he intended to come to New York, but he somehow got detained. In any event, Capone was not an active participant in the on-going conflict.

90

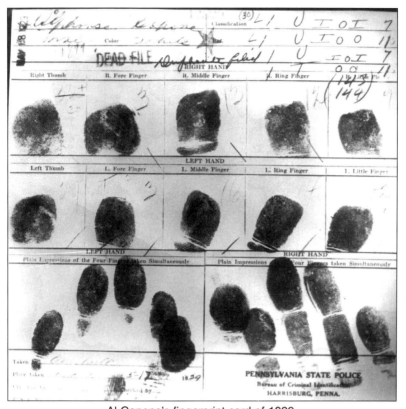

Al Capone's fingerprint card of 1929.

(PHILADELPHIA POLICE)

When Capone came to Philadelphia, neither Sabella nor any other gangster here gave the notorious criminal any recognition, any place to stay, and least of all, any safety. Capone probably expected the inhospitality. More important than Sabella's indifference, however, Capone seemed to have wanted to sabotage Masseria's plans on what he was supposed to do for him in New York. Capone had condoned Masseria's maltreatment of the Castellammaresi, Sabella's *paesani*; hence, the gangster-celebrity received no welcome from other gangsters, in apparent respect to Sabella. An anonymous call to the Philadelphia police that Capone was carrying a firearm

91

illegally resulted in his arrest on May 17, 1929. Capone was then, protected.

Sabella seemed not to consider Capone a guest of Philadelphia's underworld. If Sabella was either already in New York to aid his fellow Castellammaresi or preparing to leave Philadelphia as Capone entered the city, Sabella had his obligations. The boss may have felt about Capone the same way as Bonanno and others regarded the Neapolitan who was not yet allowed to become a member of the Mafia Tradition. Capone was, nevertheless, an associate of Masseria's.[98] Found guilty, he was incarcerated at Eastern State Penitentiary in a cell which he was allowed to decorate, ordered his food to be delivered and just waited for the Sicilians to finish killing each other.

Capone owed the Sicilians some form of debt, however. He was given opportunities to expand through the Sicilians' nationwide network of contacts; they protected him; and he knew to continue to pay them respect in the form of tribute money. Capone may have suspected that there were too many Castellammaresi near him to act against them. So, he stayed in Philadelphia.

Philadelphia's Mafia Family in 1929 had only a few Castellammaresi as members; most members were from other areas in western Sicily. A review of Sabella's group shows members as well as associates which parallel other Sicilian American Mafia Families throughout the urban United States venues. All of Sabella's members were of Sicilian ancestry on the paternal as well as maternal sides. The differences that did separate these individuals were mainly on who was born of a Mafia family in western Sicily, who was not of a Mafia family but from western Sicily and, who was from eastern Sicily where no Mafia existed. Most members had no criminal records, judging from the list of about twenty identified as Sabella's crew. Some men were born in Sicily. Some arrived shortly after Mussolini's initial drive to expel Mafiosi from Sicily in 1925. Some came with their parents or alone as youngsters or teenagers. A few of the known associates from mainland Italian ancestry did have arrests on gambling, but none on assault or related offenses. These associates who traced their roots to the regions of Campania or Calabria correspond to Capone, Vito Genovese, Albert Anastasia, Frank Costello and Joseph Valachi who also were allied with Sicilian American Mafiosi during Prohibition and who subsequently became members in the hybrid La Cosa Nostra in the fall of 1931.

Because the associates willfully became a part of a formal organization as a result of the illegal liquor industry, their decisions to do so negated Ianni's "Ethnic Succession" theory that held that this latest group of immigrants or first generation native-born followed the same course of a small minority of Irish and Jewish gangsters in previous decades.[99] By the 1920s, the Sicilian American Mafia had been functioning for almost forty years in Philadelphia. Moreover, the 1928 inquest also never identified any of Sabella's members or associates as the area's leaders in alcohol sales and distribution. It was to be a choice made by a bootlegger: to be independent or to engage within a wider network of operations that introduced him to Sicilians who ran one of these organizations. Gradually, cultural affinity declined in relation to the earnings potential of the associates. Indeed, as Alan Block noted, the Sicilian American Mafia's structure and function was not as "informal" or "parochial" during the 1920s to warrant modification.[100] With Sabella's Family and their extensions, as with other Families in, for example, New York and Chicago, there were associates of mainland Italian ancestry, Eastern European (Jewish) descent and the demands of a hetergeneous, native-born public that contributed to a wider scope of social as well as criminal interactions at this time.

Sabella was one of only a few from Philadelphia who either knew or was acquainted with Salvatore Maranzano, Masseria's opponent. To Joseph Bonanno, Maranzano was like a god in Castellammare del Golfo.[101] Many of Sabella's and his wife's relatives and friends now fought under him without hesitation. To Gentile, Sabella and his men took part in what he called Maranzano's "band of Pancho Villa."[102] Of the five Mafia Families in New York, only the Profaci Family remained neutral, as the others allied themselves with either Masseria or Maranzano. Law enforcements' official records on the Castellammarese War are mostly unreliable and incomplete. Gentile recalled that the New York *capo* of police gave Masseria an ultimatum: the Sicilians could carry out their "war" if it did not harm innocent citizens.[103] New York City's newspapers, knowing of the conflicts, had met and published pleas to the gangsters to try to spare those not involved in the underworld dispute.[104] It was then expected that police in every jurisdiction would focus on the average citizen of New York while trusting gunfire to intended victims.

The thirty-eight year old Sabella and his crew of about nine[105] went to New York for Maranzano while the remaining members in Philadelphia oversaw Family interests. There is no significance to this number sent to fight. Hess recited information that Mafiosi used to be divided into groups of ten, led by a *capo di diecina*.[106] Antonino Calderone's later testimony furthered the description of the *decina* boss which was more akin to the "captain" rank of late, one of subordination to the underboss, as well as to the boss.[107] But with Sabella's Family, this number may only represent the available number of Mafiosi competent to fight versus those who had to stay and to administer affairs in Philadelphia, which accounted for about twenty (20).

Gentile described the Castellammaresi's part in the war as nothing short of continuous killings of those of

Sicilian, including Castellammarese, ancestry, and mainland Italians. Disputes over the number of fatalities in this conflict which began in 1927 and ended in late 1931 arose mainly because of the problem of material evidence.[108] The range of battlefields also was broad, beyond New York, with some bodies presumably unidentified, unclaimed or, in unknown places. None of the "Greasers" were particularly targeted[109] and elderly Mafiosi held their own. Maranzano, at age sixty-two ordered one of Masseria's high-ranking men to be killed as a sign of his bid for absolute power.[110] It was anticipated that the death of Peter "Clutch Hand" Morello, Masseria's underboss, in August of 1930 would have signalled to his Family a halt in the war. "Don Pitru," as he was called, was the brains to Masseria's force, wrote Joseph Bonanno, a Castellammarese and Sabella's *paesano*.[111] Gentile held that "Massaria" wanted peace, but Maranzano was unwilling to talk.[112] "Clutch Hand's" killing though, proved nothing but heartache for his family. At least another year of bloodshed trailed behind efforts to stop, against the opportunities to usurp the deceaseds' holdings.

To some, the deaths among the Sicilians meant imminent social change when the Organization that had been for centuries sustained in the medieval culture of western Sicily would exist no more in the United States. It is apparent that the Sicilian American Mafiosi knew this then because this generation of men, including Maranzano (born in 1868) and Masseria (born in 1880) and Sabella (born in 1891) as well as many, many others never recommended their sons to be Mafiosi in the United States. In fact, the sons of the two commanders of the Castellammarese Wars, both adults, were spared any wartime service as they were neither associates nor involved in their fathers' Mafia affairs.[113]

Nonetheless, the sons would have to answer to the police and news media, comfort their mothers and bury their fathers.

Joe the Boss was shot in April of 1931 while he was eating at a Coney Island restaurant. No one saw his killer's face, but the get-a-way car was found later, leading to little, to the police's dismay.[114] "Lucky" Luciano later claimed his involvement and assumed leadership of Masseria's family.[115] It was the first LCN Family to have as its leader an individual who was not from a Mafia Tradition in Sicily. Luciano, who learned to become a gangster in the streets of New York, landed in a former Sicilian American Mafia Family that was in serious crisis[116] and used his street smarts to resolve it.

"No one won...there was just peace," said one of Sabella's men who went with him to New York. It was a statement that was typical of the mindset of the Friends who fought and survived to recollect about the war. Friends, unanimously, without hesitation and without trying to make a sanitized version of what actually happened conceded on the result but were wont to gloat over triumphs that ended at various times for different Families.[117] One Philadelphia Mafioso stayed with Sabella for almost two years but it is uncertain if Sabella and his crew participated in the full four and one-half years of conflict. What is certain is that the function and ideology of the Organization definitely changed.

• • • • • • • • •

Retired from the Mafia...at age forty
● ●

Salvatore and Maria Sabella, along with their six children had sold their Philadelphia businesses, suburban home and moved to a safe section in Brooklyn for the war. They lived on a street with "Americans," transferred to New York schools and acclimated.[118] Salvatore was supposedly with the Castellammaresi who would later become names known to future law enforcement: Stefano Magaddino, boss of Buffalo, Joseph Bonanno, successor to Maranzano in New York and the names of lower-ranking members named Galante, Bonventre, Chiodo and DiGregorio. Sometime near the end of the war, Sabella was arrested in northern New Jersey for atrocious assault and battery with an automobile. When he gave his address, agents later noted that Sabella was living in what had been the home of Steve Magaddino in 1921. There, Magaddino was arrested with six others in August of 1921 for the murder of Camillo Caizzo whose body was found in a sack in New Jersey. This was the same victim in Detective Fiaschetti's book. A likely suspect to the death, Stefano probably contracted Bartolomeo Fontana who later confessed to the murder to Fiaschetti. Magaddino's brother Pietro had been killed by Caizzo and Frank Buccelatto in Castellammare del Golfo sometime between 1913 and 1916.[119] Stefano never experienced the proper redress in 1921; in 1931, Sabella's *paesani* posted his bail and arranged for his release. He was given a suspended sentence. When booked, Sabella told the police that he was a "butcher."[120] And like other Castellammaresi, he was never to complete his sentence.

The following month, Sabella stepped down voluntarily as the *rapprisentanti* of Philadelphia. It is difficult to assess whether Sabella's 1931 arrest made any difference to his position in the local Family or to the national Families in general. His alliance with the other Castellammaresi evidently was a benefit, but Sabella may have simply been spent by his Mafia duties. He was just forty years old when he decided to retire as an active member of the Philadelphia Mafia.

The Sicilian American Mafia, after almost fifty years of existence in the United States was regarded by then to have been obsolete, culturally and philosophically. Gentile had said that he practiced certain principles to defend honor and human justice, but these had "degenerated."[121] Friends who were accustomed to a medieval lifestyle that was incompatible with the fast-paced modern, foreign society in the United States acquiesced to change. Urban Families experienced a more abrupt change than those in the rural areas who had other types of stressors. But it was inevitable—the Organization was now different—it finally evolved.

Sabella stepped down gracefully, and no one was uncomfortable. The criminal charges of 1927 and 1931 may have added cumulatively to the toll of reasons why Sabella was overwrought with pressures. He had become a figure to be investigated by an inquiring news media, a fixer, a father, a spouse, business partner and a very exhausted man by the end of 1931. In September of 1931, Salvatore Maranzano was stabbed and shot multiple times in his New York office. His assailants left hats that bore the labels of Chicago stores. The sixty-three year old Maranzano, called by *The New York Times* a "Smuggler of immigrants" tried to wrestle the four assailants off only to die a slow death by the stiletto and pistol. Assuming Maranzano's end, just days before, Al Capone surfaced in the city and asked the elevator operator where Maranzano's office was located.[122]

Salvatore Sabella though, remained a member, albeit a passive one, of what was the local LCN and at first only observed the new Organization's Families that had some new faces and varied cultural attitudes. His successor was John Avena, whom Sabella had mentored and grown to accept as more than a Friend.[123] But Sabella noticed what the new members to the local Family brought with them from their mainland Italian cultures. Now, men from the Naples and Reggio Calabria areas were members after years as associates. Meetings were now spoken in Italian rather than in Sicilian. Gambling was now one of the Family's income-producing activities. There were rumors that illegal narcotics and prostitution were businesses of younger members with gangster backgrounds. John Avena may have been able to challenge these men and their practices, but Sabella apparently was not.

After the Castellammarese War, Sabella resettled in the Philadelphia suburbs with his wife and children. He owned more legitimate businesses and retained "soldier" status with the Family in order to have low or no responsibility and some mutual respect among other members. During this time, in the early 1930s, Sabella, along with John Avena and A. Domenico Pollina finally did go to trial in the Zanghi-Cocozza murders. Count Judge Lamberton among others in Philadelphia's judiciary who were in collusion with the local Mafia:[124] in just one day, on March 7,

Leaders in Grand Jury War on Crime

This photograph, taken outside the Grand Jury room in City Hall yesterday, shows District Attorney Monaghan, at right and Harry Diller, foreman of the Grand Jury that is conducting a searching investigation of crime in Philadelphia.

(PUBLIC LEDGER)

1933, all three Sicilian Friends were found "not guilty" of two counts of first degree murder,[125] proving that the Mafia's power still silently stretched into the Philadelphia Police and District Attorney's Office. Another Mafia leader, John Avena would influence the same civil servants, law enforcement and criminal justice system in Philadelphia as his predecessors.

These blatant, repetitive instances of corruption and collusion may explain why the Pennsylvania Crime Commission reports had continued to present nothing but untruths in their "history" of Philadelphia's Mafia and La Cosa Nostra. Except for the correct spelling of his name and his presence at a "gunfight in May of 1927 in which two persons were killed,"[126] his arrest and acquittal, the remaining information published in these reports about Sabella does not square with the FBI's findings, the newspaper and public records and testimonies from Sabella's family and Friends. (Refer to Appendix III.) In retrospect, if indeed the Sicilian American Mafiosi in this city were less overtly violent than other gangsters and were limited in their criminal involvements to alcohol-related activities, paid protection, loan sharking and various types of negotiating for pay, it would make sense for law enforcement and civil servants to be influenced. But it would also be prudent to divulge this fact of Philadelphia's history at this stage of the local Family's evolution in order to correlate it with other urban centers of Mafia activity during Prohibition.

The Sabella family moved again to New York in 1934, not intending to stay too long. Although Salvatore Sabella seemed at that time to be somewhat "retired" from the Mafia, there were still some loose ends that had to be tied. By coincidence, at the same time that Sabella was residing in Brooklyn with his wife and six children, Anthony "Musky" Zanghi was also in New York, alone, just dining in a restaurant. Sabella may have had moments of recall over the years, remembering Zanghi at City Hall on the evening of May 30, 1927...the subsequent pay-off to keep Zanghi quiet about underworld activities...the Zanghi gang's murder of George Catania...and there must have been many, many other unpublicized incidences of Zanghi's misdeeds in the neighborhood.

It was August of 1934 and nothing had changed with Zanghi. He never "went straight." He never left Philadelphia permanently either after the Mafia's huge pay-off. In fact, all of the Mafia money paid to Zanghi never did anything to halt his career of crime throughout Philadelphia. Over half of Zanghi's brief life of 34 years was spent in criminal mischief. Somehow, in October of 1928, Musky had escaped from another murder rap, that of Anthony Denni, which occurred, by coincidence, on the opposite corner of Eighth and Christian Streets where Joey and Scabby were shot.[127] The Philadelphia Homicide Police had first named Musky as the murderer of Anthony Denni in October of 1928 at 804 Christian Street; then, the homicide record had "unsolved" scribbled next to Zanghi's undeleted name. The killing remains a mystery.

Anthony "Musky" Zanghi's offenses were made to seem as if he "just happened" to be there by mistake, or "just happened" to be erroneously identified as an alleged killer. By 1934, with numerous contracts out on his life, and not all by Mafiosi, no one could guess who would take Musky out first. Today, there are those who still recall his resumé of crime: bigamist, cop killer, thief and most likely, a murderer.[128]

But appearances at crime scenes were more than a coincidence.

Zanghi left that New York City restaurant bullet-riddled.

No one ratted on Zanghi's alleged killer, his friend, the contract murderer, Anthony "Stinger" Cugino who met his untimely death by hanging the following year in the same city. New York police called Cugino's jail cell demise a "suicide" though many considered the act was allegedly by Philadelphia Police Captain James Ryan. Musky's legacy had more twists of fate relative to Philadelphia's Mafiosi

Star Witness Missing

ANTHONY "MUSKY" ZANGHI,
who has mysteriously disappeared after
trial was begun of alleged slayer of his
brother and Vincent Cocozza.

Star Witness
in Gang Trial
Has Disappeared

**Musky, Who "Squealed" on
Alleged Slayers, Mys-
teriously Missing**

Bought off or Killed?

(THE PHILADELPHIA RECORD)

after his death. One prison convict named William Denni,
who previously had a "beef" with Zanghi gave a signed
statement to the authorities as his last confession before
his walk to the electric chair. Denni swore that Zanghi had
framed Luigi Quaranta in the 1927 murders—his final tes-

timony was legally sustainable. Quaranta was then freed from Eastern State Penitentiary to rejoin his Friends.[129] Thereafter, Lou Quaranta would quietly live on as a Mafioso in Philadelphia, using an old haberdashery as a "front" for his business. He would pass on naturally of old age.

After Prohibition was repealed in 1933, Sabella looked at changing careers and investments. He tried his hand at the garment industry, owning a factory and encouraging some of his children to take up tailoring and dressmaking in their youth. He was unlucky at gambling and did not become involved in the vice that was now taking precedence as the income-producing commodity in the local Family led by his old Friend, John Avena. With Prohibition repealed however, Sabella still gravitated to the stills where he was arrested in March of 1935 for "manufacturing and distilling alcohol" in Montgomery County, just outside of Philadelphia. Allegedly, some of Sabella's "Anglo-Saxon Protestant" friends bankrolled the small enterprise, but were not arrested for their involvement.[130] I have no information on why at this time Sabella was left on his own without assistance from anyone in the Organization. He may have been embarrassed. He may have wanted to save face—we do not know what the circumstances were. It was unusual for any Mafia boss, even a retired one, to be left alone, incarcerated. Evidently, the same practices of pay-offs to civil servants did not apply in suburban Philadelphia as in the city. But it is surprising that Sabella had to experience this, which leads me to believe that perhaps he did not want to contact anyone for help. One person who knew Sabella described him as "petty" and annoying to younger members and associates, a quality that worked for, as well as against him. The Montgomery County Prison records showed only Sabella's wife and brother as his visitors during his three month stay—no Friend, no other Castellammarese, no other relative or associate.[131] Whether Sabella wanted to act independently or to estrange himself from the Mafia voluntarily are only speculations. It was a fact that he was there, in prison, not because of Family business.

But would one Friend let another alone in this circumstance? It seems so in this matter. Sabella was incarcerated this time in the same suburban Philadelphia town where several established Mafiosi like "Zu Ninu" lived and were, like Sabella, from western Sicily. Some were contemporaries of Sabella only in age—these Friends were Francis Ianni's "leading businessmen," successful men in legitimately-owned factories, land speculations and stores who led their lives as Mafiosi away from the graft, bloodshed and vulgarities of the city. Unlike Sabella, excessive force and threats of physical harm rarely were used by these rural Mafiosi. One physician described his grandfather who was used as a "hostage" until disputes were settled between the Friends, an ideal to Sabella but unrealistic among the element existing in South Philadelphia.

Nick Gentile also may have provided some information on what was transpiring in the underworld in these post-Prohibition years. He recounted that Salvatore Maranzano gave an order during the Castellammarese Wars to "kill the Sciaccatani"[132] in their hometown overseas, in Sciacca, because of the alliance their New York brethren had with "Joe the Boss" Masseria. Maranzano lived for only about five years in the United States and may not have known where Sciaccatani colonies were located outside of New York, which proved to be to Sabella's disadvantage. In 1935, Sabella would find himself imprisoned in one of the oldest and largest Sciaccatani strongholds in the United States. He might have figured that he was probably safer behind bars than among those whom his *paesano* had condemned to die.

Sabella was still somewhat disassociated from his former Family in the 1930s when a Mafia tragedy struck. Leaving behind responsibilities, and with a pronounced disinterest in the current bookmaking/gambling industry that took precedence after alcohol no longer served as the local Family's primary form of income, Sabella spent more time outside of Philadelphia. His successor, John Avena had formed alliances with members of the Jewish Mob that had ties that ran from Philadelphia through New Jersey to New York and points between in a major bookmaking operation. The same members in the "Jewish Mob," or "69th Street Mob" however, also knew and often associated with the Lanzettis, the Philadelphia Mafia's antagonists. It was a rather flammable underworld environment which Sabella apparently recognized and sought to avoid. But as testy as these La Cosa Nostra members, Jewish gangsters and Lanzettis may have been, no one would have surmised that one of the Lanzettis would imprudently act out.

Salvatore Sabella, boss of Philadelphia during eleven of Prohibition's thirteen years of blood and corruption said goodbye to his Friend, John Avena who at age forty-three died by a spray of bullets where Washington and Passyunk Avenues cross at the "Bloody Angle." Several months later, Sabella would hear of the Friends' revenge on the Lanzetti brothers. Then years later, more revenge on the Lanzettis.

Philadelphia's retired Mafia boss settled permanently in the suburban counties by the late 1930s with his six children, mostly teenagers, and his wife. Total separation from his Friends in downtown South Philadelphia in these years in the 1940s was impossible as Sabella in middle age realized on whom he could depend for friendship and company. He saw the changes in this new kind of organization with those of mainland Italian lineage admitted as members— Avena had initiated many Italians and many who were as himself, from eastern Sicily with no Mafia Tradition and who learned about the Family and their ways secondhand. Sabella's Friends Restucci, Fusci, Girgenti and Macaluso also became inactive and never passed the Mafia Tradition on to their sons or nephews, just as the Montgomery County, New Orleans and most New York Mafiosi who were born of the Honored Society's families in western Sicily. Their Mafia was in a silent, unwritten history now.

However this did not suggest that Sabella and whatever he was doing was not documented by others. The FBI noted that the former boss was seen regularly in South Philadelphia while the Philadelphia Police claimed it was daily. The frequent visits to Friends and former associates brought curiosity even from Sabella's sons who now became interested in their father's close circle of male companions. Any hint of inquisitiveness in these Friends and their obsessive interest in gambling was quickly countered by the father who admonished his sons never to familiarize themselves with their father's Friends. The defensiveness though, did elicit more curiosity, especially with regards to the gambling, but Sabella became stricter. Sabella wanted his boys to be "American" and was proud to claim his three sons as veterans of World War II. When his brother-in-law was arrested for gambling in 1941, an entirely preventable offense in Philadelphia, the Sabellas, as parents, did not want this incident to be known to the children. Salvatore and Maria instilled in their children the differences between right and wrong and taught them that an arrest was not to be condoned—it was a disgrace, not a "badge of honor" nor a run of bad luck to have been caught at a crime, said their offspring. However it was difficult for the maturing Sabella teenagers in the 1940s not to be aware of their father's arrests. Sabella's one arrest as a "disorderly person" was satisfied with a paid fine of $7.50 and was regarded as an extremely minor infraction to the authorities. But it still was a crime. And on record.[133] A raid by the

Philadelphia Police justified neighbors' suspicions of a row-house on Eighth near Montrose Street as "being (the) head-quarters of a 'numbers syndicate'"[134] in which Sabella and others were apprehended, then discharged. He was not merely at the wrong place at the wrong time. Sabella's presence was obvious for his association with known book-making and gambling operators who were now working under Joseph Bruno, né Dovi, who ran Philadelphia from his home in New Brunswick, New Jersey. An avid gambler himself and someone who had long known how the Republican machine governed law and politics in Philadelphia, Bruno apparently influenced this dismissal of the charges against his long-time Friend, Sabella.

But Bruno's hands were tied beyond state and local offenses: The last arrest somehow led Sabella to the Federal authorities, namely the Immigration and Naturalization Service, a branch of the Department of Justice. Shortly after the gambling raid, the INS notified the retired Mafioso that he was in default for failing to comply with the Alien Registration Act of 1940.[135] By then, Sabella's Mafia liability was more attractive to Federal law enforcement. This was quite unexpected. In the era after the Castellammarese Wars and repeal of the Eighteenth Amendment there still existed in Philadelphia a relationship between local law enforcement and the underworld unlike in most of the major urban centers in the United States. Comparatively, however, the criminal element from the Italian and Sicilian ethnos in Philadelphia's gangland was not part of the criminal profile as it had been in New York or in Chicago where arrests in the 1930s of Mafia/LCN members and other males of Italian ancestry were seemingly in greater numbers. Any individual can see in the numerous crime histories or in the many journalistic-type accounts of "mob histories" or "encyclopedias" of American Mafiosi that in the 1930s, when Luciano, Genovese and

Capone, among others, were repeatedly arrested and incarcerated, they have no contemporaries of Italian or Sicilian ancestry in Philadelphia.[136] In the 1940s, the same trend continued with most local LCN members remarkably evading felonies and never seeming to attract the news media in the same capacity as their counterparts in New York, Chicago and the cities with lesser populations, but with comparable Families (Kansas City, Cleveland, Detroit, Buffalo and Boston.) Angelo Bruno was arrested during the 1940s for gambling, but no civil servant or news reporter made much of this LCN member or his Friends, possibly due to the tradition that "grandfathered" Philadelphia Mafiosi for almost fifty years.

Nevertheless, the case of Salvatore Sabella possesses some breaks with the past. Again, in the 1940s, he was charged with "larceny and receiving stolen goods"—about $830.00 worth of nylon hose allegedly was never delivered to the buyer who filed the matter with the state court. A few months later, a "nolle pros" was entered on the dockets and Sabella was cleared.[137] But these acts, however, more frequent now in Sabella's midlife than before, lead one to wonder about Sabella's willingness to perpetrate crime beyond the victimless offenses of alcohol manufacturing and gambling, and the traditional Mafia crimes of loan-sharking and paid protection. Eventually, federal law enforcement reviewed Sabella's record of arrests and found an adult male who was a repeat offender of more felonies than misdemeanors.

Sabella had lost a considerable amount of money in the 1930s due to bona fide investments that unpredictably failed. The family was not wealthy, but it was middle-class, and the Sabella children had a strong work ethic. Unlike others in the Philadelphia Family, Sabella had no diversified sources of income as did the LCN Friends in the city who owned bars, clubs, restaurants, factories, trucking and construction companies, and supplemented them with the bookmaking and other gambling profits. Other members sidelined their legitimate businesses with illegal narcotics and prostitution by the mid- to late 1930s, taking a lead from John Avena's successor, Joseph Bruno.

Law enforcement's interest in the aging Salvatore Sabella did arise on a number of occasions from the "Little Italy" residents who complained about him. Sabella's visits to the neighborhood infuriated many who obviously did not pay heed to the Mafia Tradition and Sabella's former rank. On another report taken on Sabella, one "Little Italy" businessman told law enforcement about a storeowner who was forced to close because he allegedly competed with one of Sabella's interests there in the 1940s. Joe Bruno again was asked to intervene and was said to have paid the storeowner compensation for Sabella's indiscretion.[138] It is difficult to prove these allegations, and law enforcement's stance on this particular incident was neutral possibly because it was "hearsay" and quite after the fact. Sabella's family admitted that he had a meat store in the suburbs in the 1940s while he told law enforcement that he lived on the 800 block of Dickinson Street and owned a candy store.[139] Several appearances by Sabella at the INS did, however continue from the 1940s through to the 1950s.[140] During that time, Sabella's old Friend, Joe Bruno died of cardiac complications. Bruno had known Sabella from the 1920s. He was reliable and loyal to Sabella from the years before he was part of the back-up crew in the Zanghi-Cocozza murders to his premature natural death. Joe Ida, close friend and Friend of Joe Bruno, next assumed the "boss" title, though he administered the Philadelphia Family from afar. Ida, just as his predecessor Joe Bruno, maintained tangential ties to Sabella but was unable to secure the same relief for the former boss on the federal level. Sabella's visits to the INS alerted agents in the other

Justice Department's office that he was someone of interest. Fettered by continuous suspicions, Sabella contributed
to the causes of the federal offices by once admitting that
his wife's cousin was the same Stefano Magaddino, formerly of New York City, then later boss of the Buffalo, New
York Mafia Family. A "relationship investigation" soon followed to try to connect Sabella with other known
Castellammaresi with criminal records or who were suspected to be LCN members.[141] Farther afield, the Chicago
FBI also had placed Sabella with the Capone Family, which
would have greatly surprised the former *rapprisentanti*[142]
who had nothing kind to say about "Scarface." As a soldier,
Sabella was getting more attention from law enforcement
than when he was the leader of the Philadelphia Family.
Years of investigations and appearances at the INS culmi-
nated when in 1954 the agency found the sixty-three year
old Mafioso eligible for deportation because he had told the
investigator of his guilt as a juvenile offender in the 1905
murder in Sicily. Agents later concurred; but they eventually placed Sabella's case in non-priority status because of
his "age, his family and his poor health."[143]

The former Sicilian American Mafia boss was a grandfather by that time, inactive as a member but as a butcher,
asking customers what choice cut of meat they wanted. He
was a courteous man in his small town community. In the
suburbs, Salvatore Sabella had an "excellent reputation,"
his American neighbors told inquiring federal agents.[144] He
appeared to be a normal businessman who was loved by his
wife and children, the opposite of the perceptions of South
Philadelphia residents. Sabella was especially fortunate at
this time not to have been a part of the contentious events
in the city in the early 1950s. Two concurrent investigations involved the underworld and their associates, including local law enforcement and politicians. Judge Edwin O.
Lewis who presided over the 1928 police corruption case in

Stefano Magaddino

(FAMILY PHOTO)

Philadelphia would again be pressed into the same position, only now with far more criminations. The other inquest was on the national level. Initiated by Democrat Senator Estes Kefauver of Tennessee, a committee was selected to look into gambling, racketeering and organized crime all over the United States. Federal grand juries would soon be assembled in every venue where the rackets were known to operate.

In Philadelphia, the Kefauver Committee's investigation was headed by attorney Alfred M. Klein. He was startled, he said, that "Persons I had never seen or heard of telephoned or came into my office to volunteer information about numbers games, horse race bookmaking and the drug traffic."[145] Within about six months, the Kefauver Committee was then investigating Philadelphia's judiciary and police force for evidence of graft and corruption. Some police officers committed suicide at the double-dose of pressure.

Investigators for the U.S. Senate Committee in Philadelphia were given a list of names "known to have taken part in the drug traffic between New York, the racketeers' chief source of supply, and Philadelphia."[146] The only individuals named were David Glass, Samuel (Cappy) Hoffman, Harry Stromberg, Marco Reginelli and Willie Weisberg.[147] Sabella's retirement proved an advantage, at least in a city where the Mafia's existence still was not official.[148] In 1951, the local Kefauver Committee chair, Alfred Klein went abroad, spending three days interviewing the deported Salvatore "Lucky" Luciano in Italy. "Sure, there's a Mafia," said the exiled gangster who added the "worldwide" dimension to the organization.[149] Still, in Philadelphia, with two interrelated investigations, the local LCN Family remained unharmed and undisturbed by inquiries.

Maria Sabella's cross was probably more heavy than her husband's was with the Mafia. Salvatore would leave her with the six children while he would attend to his Family responsibilities sometimes for months. After Prohibition, Salvatore's finances gradually dwindled and he was never on stable ground again. Maria's ingenuity and strength held the family together when income was uncertain. She and the children would repair old homes for resale and do other jobs to maintain their level of comfort. They had two sons well over six feet tall for heavy work and the youngest's creativity and intellect to push their parents from one investment to another in real estate. The three daughters provided financial assistance as well with the warmth only females can muster.

Salvatore Sabella

(ARTIST'S ENHANCEMENT OF PHOTO FROM
THE U. S. DEPT. OF JUSTICE, FBI)

Sabella's thick curly hair only turned white in his golden years. He still had that bold stance as a senior citizen and still frequented Philadelphia's "Little Italy" neighborhood where he was still visible, perhaps the most visible Mafia boss in the 1920s, '30s, '40s and '50s. Sabella had a photographic memory that astounded anyone who tested him. He read avidly in English although he retained his accent that made some English vowels sound unintelligible. He preferred to speak half in Sicilian and half in English.

In terms of whether Sabella was characteristic of the "old" Sicilian American Mafia, he displayed only a few of the traits of the classic Mafioso. Whereas Joseph Bonanno, Joseph Profaci, Carlo Gambino and a few others born in western Sicily and descended from Mafiosi had more predictable personalities and responded to prostitution, extortion, narcotics, the Roman Catholic Church and Mafia Tradition congruously, Sabella was not wholly in tandem. Unlike those born of Mafia families in Sicily, Sabella possessed none of the poise to remain within the Organization in some active capacity. His contemporaries, Sicilians Joseph Profaci of New York, Russell Bufalino of northeastern Pennsylvania, Raymond Patriarca of Providence, Rhode Island, and those who were his peers during the Castellammarese Wars, Vito Genovese, Frank Costello and Joe Ida, were still active, still entertaining requests for more legal and illegal income-producing partnerships, and still interested in the maintenance of the mechanism within the Organization. Sabella, unlike the aforementioned, also never became involved or initiated diversified investments to maintain his own financial stability. The New Yorkers, as well as some Philadelphia Mafiosi, such as Mario Riccobene, Sr. would consider it an insult to their masculinity to depend on others or to ask for money. These Mafiosi knew that they were born *mafiusu* and had to die *mafiusu*, with respect and deserved honor. Indeed, any honorific tribute to the ideal or classic Mafioso, the *mafiusu* Mafioso in Philadelphia belonged to Michael Maggio, not Sabella. And it would not be without many reasons to evaluate Sabella's Mafia Family retrospectively to find that it had already represented a degeneration of the Mafia and the Mafia Organization unlike other Families in the United States.

Because of his visibility, as well as his accessibility, Sabella was never forgotten by the local Friends who remembered that he once was at the top rung of the hierarchal ladder. He might have been present at LCN meetings to meet newer and much younger members. Sabella knew that the 1957 meeting at Joseph Barbera's home in Apalachin, New York was "to clean up the drugs in the Organization."[150] FBI agents were told that Friends were giving Sabella weekly gifts of $200.00.[151] Angelo Bruno would visit him, "Don Turiddu" with cartons of cigarettes or other forms of "respect."[152] But outside of the confines of honor from his Mafia/LCN Friends, the fact that Sabella was seen and heard in Philadelphia's "Little Italy" so frequently made him the likely topic of conversations and gossip. Sabella's successor, John Avena, had only lived until 1936, a boss for just about five years. But Joe Bruno, who took over at Avena's death, rarely came to Philadelphia as did Joe Ida when he became boss in 1946. Still, during this time, Sabella was seen and heard in South Philadelphia. The Philadelphia Police silently surveilled the retired former boss in the company of the "Greasers" around Eighth and Christian, then Tenth and Christian Streets during the 1950s. FBI agents used to see Sabella "daily" in South Philadelphia and made a list of the "Greaser racketeers," a moniker which law enforcement used several decades too late.[153] Whether local or federal, law enforcement by this time had many willing informants in South Philadelphia to pass on the gossip, rumors and often first-hand accounts on Sabella.

It was said that in the spring of 1950, just as in the spring of 1927, "Don Turiddu's" character as a Mafioso was questioned. Although this time the disrespect to Sabella came indirectly, unlike in 1927, the gossip in Philadelphia's

116

"Little Italy" held that Sabella was a disgrace of a Mafioso. Others dared to accuse him of having an affair with a neighborhood woman. They said that he failed the Mafia and cited the 1927 Zanghi-Cocozza murders as his downfall. When the Friends traced the source of this idle talk, the 1927 incident at Eighth and Christian Streets was almost reenacted, this time at Tenth and Christian Streets with the accused unspared, lying face down in the gutter, three bullets in his skull and no witnesses. Nicknamed "Pepe Longo," the large victim was shot on the spot, detectives noted. Neighbors said that they saw no one, but the vehicle with the gunmen made a safe escape, unpursued by the police. A tipster called the police and said, "There's a guy lying in a lot of blood at Tenth and Christian Streets. He looks like he's dead." An FBI report later recorded allegations that two of the participants to this "unsolved" murder would go on to become future bosses: Angelo Bruno and Philip Testa.[154]

In every photograph that I have seen of Salvatore Sabella, from his wedding portrait in 1919 to the newsmen's photos of him in the Zanghi-Cocozza matter to the color shots of him posing with his children at their marriages, his deep-set, heavy-lidded eyes would always gaze at the viewer in a way to avert one from looking longer.

He was the last Sicilian American Mafia *rapprisentanti* in Philadelphia.

The U.S. Government established independent organized crime units in local police departments, state law enforcement offices and at the FBI by the early 1960s. Angelo Bruno's arrest in 1961 yielded Sabella's name, address and telephone number in his little address book, leading agents through a comical quest to find out who this person named, "Don Terudie" was in suburban Philadelphia.[155] The agents reasoned the "Don" was short

117

for Donald, Donato or Dominic. The telephone number was dialed but the respondent said there was no one named "Don" there and no one with the surname, "Terudie." The Sabellas never knew Salvatore as having the title, "Don"— he was "Dad" or "Pop."

It was therefore, a realization of late, and one of deep reflection of times past, without the slightest indication to be forewarned, that the remaining Sabella children would learn of their father's "other life" and their Mafia heritage through television. Some childhood memories began to surface with the conflicting ones that had the parents always reminding the children of what was right and what was wrong. The values taught to these offspring were suddenly in contrast with the public's perception of the father, the family, the relatives, their western Sicilian culture and then, the Mafia.

But that is only what it is, the Sabella children reckoned—a perception. They had raised Salvatore Sabella's grandchildren in loving homes to be white-collar professionals and taught Salvatore's next generation the same values to be good citizens. The Mafia is too foreign, too incompatible and too incomprehensible for them. "Let sleeping dogs lie," said one of Sabella's elderly children of the research conducted on the father, not willing to let the father's legacy weigh on the descendants.

But what of this Mafia heritage? Was it within Sabella to pass on? And did Sabella experience the lifelong prestige that only Mafiosi have? Henner Hess wrote that a Mafioso's reputation, with accompanying prestige were based on the Mafioso's "own actions, the attribution to him [the Mafioso] and the authority and respect enjoyed by the Mafioso type...transferred to the individual."[156] Giuseppe Genco Russo, a Mafioso in western Sicily told social reformer Danilo Dolce of the Mafia pedigree in 1960: "I was born that way...No matter who asks me a favor, I'll do him the favor because, I believe, that is what my nature prescribes to me...I am neither vain nor ambitious."[157] Another Sicilian Mafioso, Calogero Vizzini said of the Mafioso's distinction in 1958: "The fact is...that in any society there must be a category of persons who put things right again when they have become complicated."[158] They were typical Mafiosi.

• • • • • • • • •

Conscientious FBI agents had just missed Salvatore Sabella in active life but were able to obtain substantial information about him, ironically, from other Mafia/LCN members whose identities were known only in confidence with the Bureau. Some of the FBI's records on Sabella had been jumbled with inconsistencies, but were later corrected with the Friends' assistance.

Salvatore Sabella died in a local hospital in 1962 of chronic myocarditis and pulmonary emphysema, prompted by years of smoking.[159] Angelo Bruno, then-boss of the Philadelphia Family respectfully attended the very humble burial of his Friend and elder. It would be Bruno's last time to see the *rapprisentanti* who by Bruno's own spelling error, gave him another alias.

• • • • • • • •

Appendix I

The Montgomery County Sicilians and Francis A. J. Ianni, Ph.D.

● ●

I have attempted to present in this history a portrait of "the rural Mafioso", a character still known and often missed in suburban Philadelphia. Francis A. J. Ianni, Ph.D., currently associated with Columbia University in New York, was the first to document, albeit a misrepresentation, these Mafiosi whom he called "Italian-Americans in organized crime." Some clarification is deserved. (See Figure 1.)

Ianni claimed his "chief informant and constant companion in Norristown" was the "old physician from northern Italy." No one in Norristown would doubt this individual's identity because he was the most beloved and known doctor in the large western Sicilian colony. The doctor's daughter married one of my cousins, and the doctor lived in the couple's home. It was therefore a rather simple matter to confirm that Ianni met the doctor. There was, however, only one interview between the doctor and Ianni, I learned, who was then a graduate student working on his doctoral dissertation, "The Acculturation of the Italo-

Appendix I

On the Methods Used in This Study

system. All of my playmates and peers were within one or two years of my own age. Each neighborhood had its "corner," and each corner its series of age-graded gangs. Most of the other kids in my street gang were the youngest children in immigrant families in which the parents were really of my grandparents' generation. Since the younger gang always clung to the periphery of the next higher age-grade gang, I was at a disadvantage because I did not have an older brother in that next age-grade to look after my interests. As a result I moved back and forth between two separate street gangs and eventually, in about the sixth grade, I began going around with American boys from school. Then I went off to college and into the Navy, and left the colony for good.

After finishing college in 1949 with a degree in psychology, I began graduate work in sociology and anthropology. At that time Italian-Americans in anthropology were still enough of a rarity that when the time came to select the topic of my master's thesis the only question seemed to be *which* area of Italian-American acculturation to select. My adviser and I settled on a study of the rate of intermarriage with non-Italians as an index of acculturation, using my own home colony of Wilmington as the field situation. My doctoral dissertation was a field study of residential and occupational mobility as indices of acculturation among the Italian-Americans in Norristown, Pennsylvania. Norristown, which is a small industrial city just outside of Philadelphia, was my first real contact as an anthropologist with Italian-Americans in organized crime. A large proportion of the Italian-Americans there had come from the city of Sciacca on the western coast of Sicily. My chief informant and constant companion in Norristown was an old physician from northern Italy who had emigrated before the First World War. He commented in great detail and with some scorn on the habits and beginnings of the leading Sicilian-American businessmen in Norristown. All were related by blood or marriage, and he spoke darkly of blood feuds which had decimated families until marriage tied the enemies together. He traced the intricate, overlapping kinship and business relationships among them and insisted that the "mentality of the Sicilian race" made it impossible for them to think of any group larger than the family or to accept the rule of law. Therefore, each family made its own law and its men their own destiny.

Since completing the Norristown study, I have done a number of field studies of acculturation in this country and in Italy. My interest in studying Italian-American criminal syndicates, however, came only partially out of this background.

Origins of the Study

From 1958 to 1961 I taught and studied in Ethiopia, and developed a lively interest in secret societies, their internal organization, and their external

Figure 1: page 177 of *A Family Business.*

124

Americans in Norristown, Pennsylvania: 1900-1950."
(Pennsylvania State University, 1952) The doctor's daughter, Anne R. Fabbri, Director of the Paley Design Center at
Philadelphia University was sent a copy of page 177 from
Ianni's *A Family Business: Kinship and Social Control in
Organized Crime*, (New York: Russell Sage Foundation,
1972), and was asked to comment. She wrote that
"Regarding the Sicilian American businessmen and their
family customs, my father never mentioned 'blood feuds' or
any other such aberrations. He always stressed the fact
that the Sicilians came to this country, were prodigious
workers and dedicated themselves to the goals of educating
their sons and providing for their families. I never heard
anything but praise for the courage and progress of all the
Italian immigrant groups."

I was also concerned about the statement by Ianni on
the "habits and beginnings of the leading Sicilian American
businessmen" which to Ianni meant the "blood feuds," the
arranged marriages that "tied the enemies together," and
the "intricate, overlapping kinship and business relationships" because they could have been a part of my heritage
of which I was not aware. I asked many Sicilian Americans
to enlighten me on what I may not have already known,
and found that no one else, especially those over age 65,
knew what Ianni had described. At best, the arranged marriages and business ties were a bit exaggerated, possibly
because Ianni was not acquainted with western Sicilian
middle-class culture. On the "blood feuds," there was some
confusion. Was Ianni talking about Mafiosi or non-Mafiosi
who were embroiled in disputes? Lacking any police
records in which to base some indications of the "blood
feuds" within the colony, I did not find this fact of Ianni's to
be true. Some Sciaccatani passed the "blood feuds" off as
nonsense because rather than shed blood, some nuisance
individuals just "went away" and were never seen or heard

of again. The Norristown Sciaccatani were very class-oriented and frowned upon "marrying down," a habit and practice that escaped Ianni's attention, even in his dissertation. He had placed the Sicilians in Montgomery County in the general category of "southern Italian culture" which is quite distinctive from the mainland Italian cultures and very unrelated to Ianni's own Abruzzese background.

As for how the "leading Sicilian-American businessmen" gained their advantage at a time when ethnic bias was still socially acceptable in suburban Philadelphia, there were some unexpected facts which Ianni may have found interesting. "Zu Ninu" was petitioned for citizenship and naturalization by a member of one of Montgomery County's "old money" families, who was also a well-respected member of the town's high society. This individual's name, "Corson" was on the Immigration and Naturalization Service's documents. Another Mafioso was brought into the wholesale food business by a fellow local businessman of Anglo-Saxon Protestant ancestry, and prospered well. Some Mafiosi, however, chose to live frugally and humbly, though they had some degree of wealth. These men and their identities were common knowledge in Norristown's "East End" where Sicilians knew which gentlemen got extra respect. When these Mafiosi arranged the marriages of their sons and daughters to others of the same socio-economic class, they were only looking for commonalities in living standards, lifestyles and values. Consolidating inheritances, or mending relationships from the "blood feuds," never happened. In fact, Sicilian American females held their own financially, and they rarely commingled their wealth with their husbands'.

Although Ms. Fabbri recalled her father's brief encounter with Ianni in relation to only what her father discussed with her, she denied any negative suggestions the doctor would have made to Ianni. It is possible that the professor pinned others' disparagements onto the doctor, a disgrace to one so revered by the Sicilian Americans whom he cared for in Montgomery County. "My father was very disgusted by this interview," wrote Ms. Fabbri of this one-time meeting with Ianni. Why Ianni never returned to Montgomery County to resume studies from his "introduction to organized crime" is unknown. The 1972 book featured Sicilian American families in New York with pseudonyms and very vague identities.

Ianni's credibility and his sources have since been debated by others. Gus Tyler's "Book Review of Francis A.J. Ianni's *Black Mafia: Ethnic Succession in Organized Crime*" (1974) that was published in *Crime & Delinquency* 21, April, 1975, pp. 175-180, questioned Ianni's reasoning for his "evidence." The informants used by Ianni for information were on the fringes of society: a con man, a "fence," pimp and the like. Tyler then dismissed Ianni's work, and Ianni's theory, based upon the unqualified sources. Abadinsky in *Organized Crime* (1981) and in *The Mafia in America* (1981) attacked Ianni twice. In the former work he wrote, "Ianni is not convincing" (p. 55) and cited Tyler's same concerns. In *The Mafia in America* (pp. 45-48) Abadinsky again pitted Tyler to Ianni, but this time added Fisher's (1975) assessment that Ianni had "flights of fancy and ungrounded interpretation." (p. 46). Accused of not applying like representations in his sampling to the theoretical frameworks he conceived, having abstract perceptions and choosing unqualified sources, Ianni was, however, given the opportunity in the past to study Montgomery County's "Men of Honor" whose identities were uncompromised.

He chose not to study real Mafiosi.

• • • • • • • •

Appendix II

The Pennsylvania Crime Commission Reports

●●●●●●●●●●●●●●●●●●●●●●●●●●●●●●●●●●●●●

M̲y endnotes will provide the reader with many
sources for Philadelphia's Mafia history, and especially for
Salvatore Sabella, who was for most "mob watchers" somewhat of a phantom, if one was to rely upon the
Pennsylvania Crime Commission Reports. Financed in part
by the taxpayers in the Commonwealth of Pennsylvania,
the first report to publish the history was in 1971; subsequent reports documented issues and individuals related to
organized crime in general, including motorcycle gangs.
The Crime Commission claimed cooperative interaction
with various law enforcement and criminal justice agencies, and even hired law professors and others with university status as experts. The veneer of such an office
appeared as highly respectable. Then, Attorney General of
Pennsylvania, Ernest Preate, Jr. utilized political pressure
to forestall further Crime Commission operations when he
became its target for investigation. The Crime Commission
ceased to exist by about mid-1994.

Those familiar with these Crime Commission reports may have had personal reasons to find faults in them, as well as reasons based on the reports' inane purpose and the fact-finders' intrusive accounts of non-public, on-going criminal investigations, which were, at the least, unsettling to those in law enforcement. But beyond the politics of its justification, there are historical issues involved. First, there are no sources cited in the accounts referred to in the 1970 report as "The Angelo Bruno Family Southeastern Pennsylvania" (p. 20) and the last, the 1990 "Family History," (p. 153) attached. Without the references, the civilian readers or students of history or criminology cannot verify the documented facts. Following verification of the facts, there are still no indications of the source's objectivity, context and relationship to the subject. Second, these Crime Commission reports were written after the FBI's special agents had already submitted their observations and findings in memoranda, reports, etc....Many of these FBI reports were accessible to those within organized crime law enforcement, which suggests an explanation for the Pennsylvania Crime Commission's investigators' true lack of jurisdiction. Figures 2 and 3 clearly relate how some modifications were made over the twenty year span of crime reporting. Overall, however, the accounts are still inaccurate.

3. *The Angelo Bruno Family (Southeastern Pennsylvania)*. The Cosa Nostra family currently controlled by Angelo Bruno was brought to the United States by a Sicilian immigrant named Salvatore Sabella. Convicted in 1905 of murder in Sicily, Sabella fled to the United States as a stowaway in 1911. Between 1911 and 1927 he resided in Philadelphia as an illegal alien and directed the local Mafia family. On Memorial Day of 1927, two rival racketeers were brutally slain and four others were wounded in a daylight assassination attempt. Sabella was charged with the murders, and although he was acquitted, the publicity surrounding the trial brought to light his illegal residency and he was deported to Sicily.

The next boss was Joseph Bruno (no relation to Angelo), who ruled from 1927 until 1944. His headquarters was first centered in Bristol,

Figure 2: The 1970 Report.

Family History

The Mafia in Southeastern Pennsylvania began with a gang of Sicilians led by Salvatore Sabella. Sabella, born on October 21, 1881, entered the United States as a stowaway in 1911. Sabella had been convicted of murder in Sicily in 1905 and fled to the United States. He was involved in a gunfight in May 1927, in which two persons were killed and four were wounded. He was arrested but later acquitted of the charges. However, his arrest brought his illegal residency to light, and he was deported back to Sicily. John (Nazone) Avena emerged as the new leader.

Figure 3: The 1990 Report.

Gary W. Potter and Philip Jenkins, instructors in the Administration of Justice at Pennsylvania State University in *The City and The Syndicate: Organized Crime in Philadelphia* (1985) wrote no rebuttal of the Crime Commission's histories. Instead, they took the Commission's facts to task on pages 33 to 35 with no mean effectiveness. They compared the 1970 and 1980 line of succession of bosses that began with Sabella. Then, Potter and Jenkins mentioned the dates of the bosses' tenures, but appeared befuddled at the Commission's lack of data. Their comments revealed not only confusion, but totally baseless lines of statements worthy of argument: "The killing of Zanghi and Coccozza (sic) is almost certainly the Memorial Day killing referred to by the Crime Commission—but Sabella is not mentioned by the Grand Jury." Then, "It was not for the likes of Sabella to take over an alcohol company, or a major bank, or make deals with the Reading Railroad

133

Company." (page 34). How did they arrive at such conclusions? They provided no sources. And they did not question the Commission's sources or its inconsistencies. Why?

It is alarming that no academic found any fault with the Commission's histories. It is even more disturbing that no one questioned why the Commission refused to divulge its foundations for such facts. Five corroborating newspapers provided adequate information on Sabella, the trial, testimonies and investigation of the murders that was consistent. Moreover, the FBI's file on Sabella contained almost two hundred pages and could have been obtained. Sociologically then, the answers to these issues may explain why the Pennsylvania Crime Commission and others who followed suit may have never expected their competency to be undermined.

The history of Philadelphia's Mafia and La Cosa Nostra, as noted in the first pages of this text was still rather sparse in the years from 1965 to 1990, after *The Valachi Papers*, Bonanno's *Autobiography* and a substantial volume of transcriptions from FBI wiretappings were made public to verify the existence of an LCN Family headed by Angelo Bruno. In the then-current zeal by journalists, as well as by law enforcement-related writers to print copy on popular subjects, there seemed to be some type of hazard for "truth-telling" or presenting a factually accurate history of some kind. Prevaricating weighed in with the rush to produce any likely readable report on "organized crime" or on the "Mafia" or on "La Cosa Nostra" or on the "Syndicate," which were all synonymous with criminal activities by Italian or Sicilian Americans. Pressure to justify the positions in the Pennsylvania Crime Commission offices corresponded to newly created published work. It is no coincidence that each history in the Crime Commission reports had no citations. And the authors of same were anonymous. Though Potter &

Jenkins confronted the Commission only by slight implications, and then muddled their own text with baseless comments, true scholarship, in my opinion, could have influenced a movement to override politics for a place in the advancement of crime history in Philadelphia.

• • • • • • • • •

Appendix III

Commonwealth of Pennsylvania v. Avena, et al.
● ●

In about 1993, I requested for review the entire file on *The Commonwealth* v. *Avena, et al.* This case involved the six defendants noted in the text who were accused of two counts of first degree murder. Four of the suspects were Sicilian American Mafiosi. The trial began in June of 1927 with one defendant found guilty. Two defendants' cases were continued to October of that year and found, "not guilty." The remaining three murder suspects were not on trial until March of 1933. On one day, all three Mafiosi defendants were found, "not guilty."

Today, the criminal justice and legal systems follow the same basic procedures with the preliminary hearings, various motions, witnesses' testimonies, discovery, etc.... amounting to volumes of paper. This particular case, however, was handwritten, and with an evident economy of words. Appearances and hearings were reported next to the courtrooms' numbers. There were the names of police, detectives and witnesses, including tenor Mario Lanza's father, Antonio Cocozza. District Attorney John Monaghan in June of 1927 handwrote an order finding Anthony Zanghi in contempt of court and committed him to County Prison. Below this, the district attorney again ordered Zanghi imprisoned. The names of "Little Italy" business-men who posted the bails for the defendants also appeared linking them to the Mafiosi as their associates. Verdicts were noted. The three Mafiosi's names were marked for someone's reference. Luigi Quaranta's sentence to solitary confinement for life was likewise handwritten by the judge.

But perhaps the most obvious question any lawyer would ask upon seeing this file would be: "Where's the rest of it?" The entire file consisted of one (1) sheet of paper. I was told in 1993 that this is the complete file. Or it was the file: As of March of 2000, the "file," i.e., the single sheet of paper, was unable to be located.

• • • • • • • • •

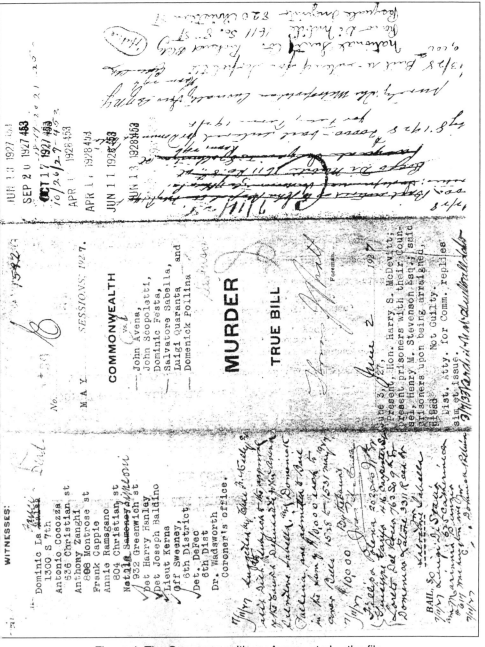

Figure 4: The Commonwealth vs. Avena, et al.—the file.

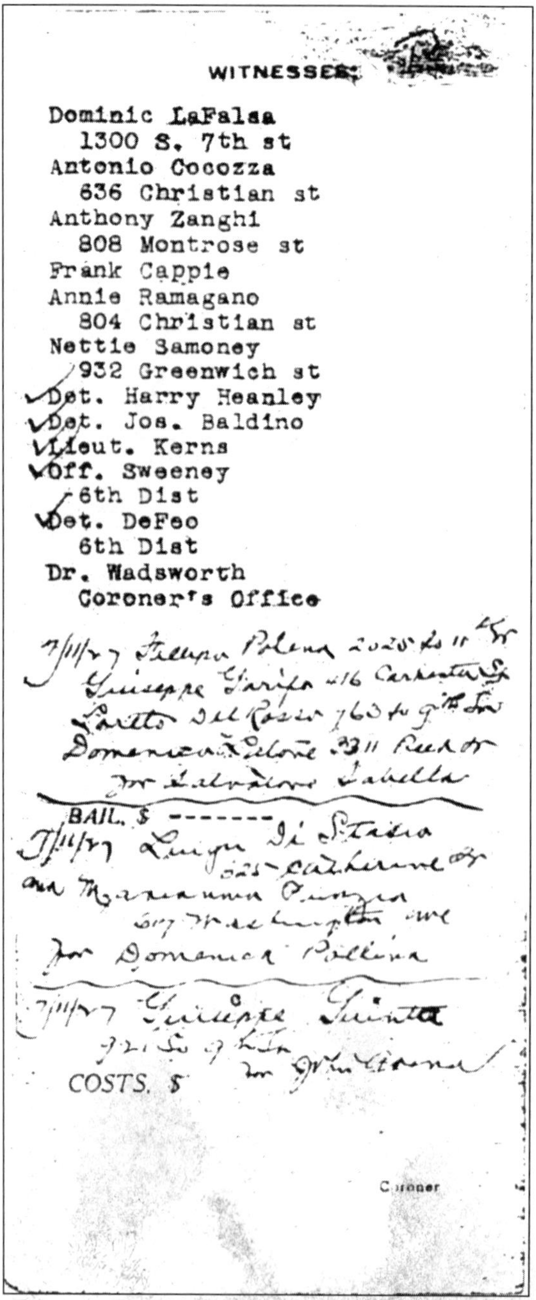

WITNESSES:

Dominic LaFalsa
1300 S. 7th st
Antonio Cocozza
636 Christian st
Anthony Zanghi
808 Montrose st
Frank Cappie
Annie Ramagano
804 Christian st
Nettie Samoney
932 Greenwich st
Det. Harry Heanley
Det. Jos. Baldino
Lieut. Kerns
Off. Sweeney
6th Dist
Det. DeFeo
6th Dist
Dr. Wadsworth
Coroner's Office

7/11/27 Filippo Polena 2020 So 11th St
Giuseppe Garifo 416 Carpenter St
Carlo Del Rosso 763 So 9th St
Domenico Delone 3311 Reed St
for Salvatore Sabella

BAIL, $ -------

7/11/27 Luigi Di Stasio
525 Catharine St
and Marianna [illegible]
507 Washington Ave
for Domenico Pollina

7/11/27 Giuseppe Guinta
921 So 9th St
for [illegible]

COSTS, $

Coroner

Figure 5: The Witness List, enlarged for legibility.

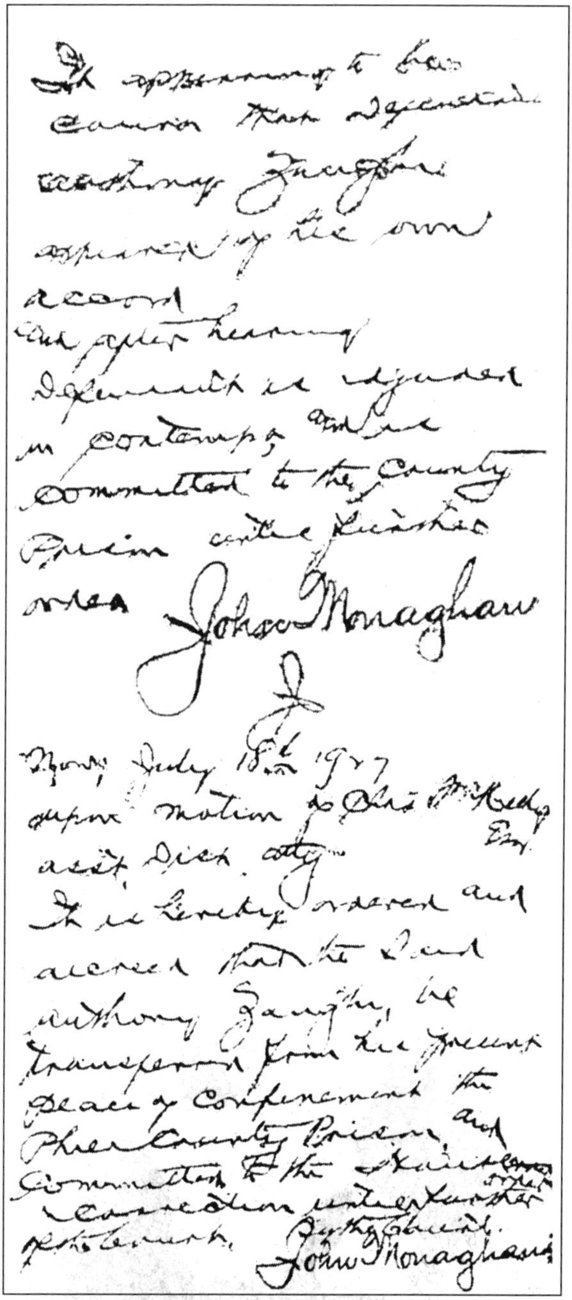

Figure 6: Judge Monaghan's Order holding Anthony Zanghi in contempt.

143

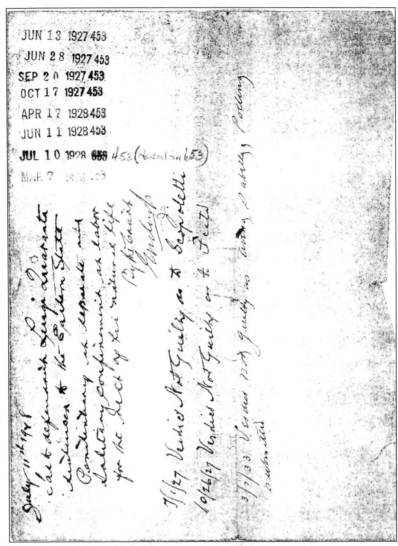

Figure 7: The Verdicts.

Notes

Notes on Historiography & Methodology
•••••••••••••••••••••••••••••••••••••

1. CHARLES H. ROGOVIN and FREDERICK T. MARTENS, "The Evil That Men Do" in PATRICK J. RYAN and GEORGE E. RUSH, Eds. *Understanding Organized Crime in Global Perspective: A Reader.* (Thousand Oaks: Sage Publications, 1997), p. 31.

2. HOWARD ABADINSKY. *Organized Crime.* (Boston: Allyn & Bacon, Inc., 1981), p. 66.

3. These include DANIEL BELL'S "Queer Ladder of Social Mobility" in "Crime as an American Way of Life" *Antioch Review* 13, Summer, 1953, pp. 131-154; FRANCIS A.J. IANNI'S "Kinship and Social Control" theory in *A Family Business: Kinship & Social Control in Organized Crime.* (New York: Russell Sage, 1972) and "The Ethnic Succession" theory in "Ethnic Succession in Organized Crime: Summary Report," National Institute of Law Enforcement and Criminal Justice, (Washington, D.C.: 1978); and PETER LUPSHA'S "Individual Choice, Material Culture and Organized Crime" in *Criminology*, Volume 19, No. 1, May , 1981, pp. 3-24.

4. ALAN BLOCK, "The History and The Study of Organized Crime." *Urban Life* 6, January, 1978, pp. 455-474.

5. DENIS MACK SMITH, *A History of Sicily: Modern Sicily After 1713.* (New York: Viking Press, 1968), p. 474.

6. FRANCIS A.J. IANNI. *A Family Business: Kinship and Social Control*, p. 177.

7. HUMBERT S. NELLI. *The Business of Crime: Italians and Syndicate Crime in the U.S.* (Chicago: University of Chicago Press, 1976) p. 169.

8. The South in particular was more expressive in ethnic bias to those of Italian ancestry. The New Orleans, Louisiana Sicilian American Mafia Families had only aroused anti-ethnic sentiments after the Hennessey shooting. Refer to RICHARD GAMBINO'S *Vendetta* (New York: Doubleday, 1977) for his work on this subject and his sources.

9. DONALD R. CRESSEY, *Theft of the Nation: The Structure and Operations of Organized Crime in America*, (New York: Harper & Row, 1969), p. ix. Also see Cressey's "Methodological Problems in the Study of Organized Crime as a Social Problem." *The Annals of the American Academy of Political and Social Science* 374, November, 1967, pp.101-112.

• • • • • • • • •

Notes to Part I
● ●

1. LEOPOLDO FRANCHETTI and SIDNEY SONNINO, *La Sicilia nel 1876*, (Florence, Italy: Vallecchi Editore, 1925), as cited in Mack Smith, p. 465.

2. MACK SMITH, pp. 474, 492 and 495.

3. Pennsylvania Crime Commission Report of 1970, p. 20 and the 1990 Report, p. 153, Last printed in Conshohocken, Pennsylvania in 1991 by the Commonwealth of Pennsylvania.

4. THOMAS M. PITKIN, *The Black Hand* (Totowa, New Jersey: Rowman & Littlefield, 1977), pp. 38-9.

5. NICK GENTILE, *Vita di Capomafia*, (Milan, Italy: Editori Riuniti, 1963), pp. 23, 60, 66 and 70.

6. Refer to GENTILE, ibid., who upon his arrival in New York was greeted by those from his hometown of Siculiana, Province of Agrigento, Sicily, pp. 23, 37-44.

7. MACK SMITH, p. 474.

8. DIEGO GAMBETTA, *The Sicilian Mafia: The Business of Private Protection.* (Cambridge: Harvard University Press, 1993), Appendix B, page 264 confirms the existence of the Mafia in Campobello di Mazara, Sicily.

9. As referenced in Gambino, pp. 186-193, Appendix P: "Report by Federal District Attorney William Grant to U.S. Attorney General William H.H. Miller, dated April 27, 1891."

149

10. Ibid., pp. 52 and 56.

11. Ibid., p. ix. Confirmed by the National Association for the Advancement of Colored People (NAACP) as the "Largest lynching in U.S. history," the deaths of these ten Sicilians and one Italian in New Orleans were, to Gambino, "Social violence and propaganda." White-on-white lynchings during the Gilded Age were indeed significant—75% of the lynchings before 1900 were white victims. Suggested readings on this issue are in STEWARD E. TOLNAY and E.M. BECK's *A Festival of Violence: An Analysis of Southern Lynchings, 1882-1930*, (Urbana: University of Illinois Press, 1995); FRANK SHAY, *Judge Lynch: His First One Hundred Years*, (New York: Ives Washburn, Inc., 1938); JAMES E. CUTLER, *Lynch-Law*, (Montclair: Patterson Smith, reprinted, 1969); WALTER WHITE, *Rope & Faqqot*, (New York: Knopf, 1929); and, EDWARD AYERS, *Vengeance & Punishment*, (New York: Oxford Press, 1984).

12. ROGER LANE, *Murder in America: A History*. (Columbus: Ohio State University Press, 1997), p. 153.

13. The DiGiovanni family was on the maternal side of "Zu Ninu's" family—a family name already publicly known in organized crime in a few sites of Mafia activity in the U.S. "Zu Ninu's" surname remains anonymous because he had no criminal record and was not later identified by law enforcement because he had long died.

14. The title, "Zu" in Sicilian corresponds to the Italian, "Zio" and literally means, "uncle," although at that time the title signified familiarity and respect to senior males. Females were called, "Za," Sicilian for "Aunt." It is not, as claimed by Gambetta, "Mafia terminology," p. 127, although Nick Gentile referred to himself as "Zu Cola," p. 32.

15. PITKIN, p. 49.

16. ANTON BLOK, *The Mafia of a Sicilian Village, 1860-1960*, (Amsterday: University of Amsterdam Press, 1972), p. 193, and MARC BLOCH, *Feudal Society*, (Chicago: University of Chicago Press, 1961), pp. 123-4, 148 and 231.

17. IANNI, p. 177.

18. PITKIN, pp. 38, 55 and 138.

19. Gentile identified "sciaccatani" numerous times in his book, e.g., on pages 25, 69, 99, 128 and 144-5.

20. PITKIN, p. 39.

21. Ibid., p. 79.

22. ANTONIO CUTRERA, *La Mafia e I Mafiosi* (Palermo: 1900), pp. 25-30 as referenced in HENNER HESS, *Mafia & Mafiosi: The Structure of Power*, (Lexington: Heath, 1970), p. 94; Gambetta, pp. 262-3; and Nelli, pp. 14-17.

23. These societies still operate in Boston, New York (Brooklyn), and outside of the Philadelphia, sites of western Sicilian colonies.

24. Cutrera, as referenced in Nelli, pp. 14-17.

25. *Stuppagghieri* is a Sicilian word intended to ridicule or to degrade someone. A related saying would be, "too big for one's britches." Nelli, pp. 14-15, claimed that this group was first recorded by Cutrera. Refer to Nelli's sources on p. 392 and for his interpretation.

26. As cited in Nelli, pp. 15-16.

27. GIUSEPPE MONTALBANO, "La Mafia e il Banditismo," *Rinascita*, October, 1953, p. 170.

28. GAMBETTA, p. 154.

29. IANNI, p. 177; Boyd's Business Directories for Montgomery County, 1880 to 1920; Personal interviews; Departments of Deeds and Real Estate, Montgomery County Courthouse, Norristown, Pennsylvania.

30. GAMBINO, p. 58.

31. CHRISTOPHER DUGGAN, *Fascism and the Mafia*, (New Haven: Yale University Press, 1989), p. 44.

32. PITKIN, p. 59. The Williamsburg section in Brooklyn was fairly middle-class Sicilian American at that time, (p. 53). PITKIN also does not identify too many prosperous Sicilians who lived on Elizabeth Street who were Black Hand victims because of their status. (p. 93)

33. Refer to the theories in Nikos Passas (Ed.), *Organized Crime*, (Brookfield: Dartmouth Publishing Company, 1995).

34. PITKIN, p. 152.

35. DUGGAN, p. 47.

36. As referenced in Duggan, p. 40, from CESARE LOMBROSO'S *L'uomo delinquente in rapporto all'antropologia, alla giurisprudenca ed alle discipline cacerarie.* (1889), and, *Le Crime: causes et remedes,* (1899).

37. *The New York Times* of July 27, 1907; August 4, August 12, November 11 and December 10, 1907.

38. Nelli, pp. 69-100.

39. *The New York Times* articles noted above.

40. PITKIN, p. 136

41. For example, in *The New York Times* accounts of August 27, 1908 and January 20, 1909, the Pennsylvania town of Scranton in the Pocono Mountain area was a site of Black Hand activities and the surrounding areas where mining camps were located.

42. *The Evening Bulletin* and *The Philadelphia Inquirer* of May 11, 1910.

43. Philadelphia Police Homicide Records Volume 4: the death of "Erneste Velpendeso" on September 21, 1914; the death of Salvatore Patti in 1921; and in Volume 7, homicide report of August 2, 1926.

44. ROGER LANE, *Violent Death in the City: Suicide, Accidents and Murder in Nineteenth Century Philadelphia*, (Cambridge: Harvard University Press, 1979), p. 102.

45. Ibid., p. 103.

46. Philadelphia Police Homicide Reports in Volumes 1,3,4 and 5, noting homicides from 1892 to 1919; not inclusive is Volume 2, now lost, which documented deaths from 1909 to 1914.

47. NELLI, pp. 69-100.

48. GENTILE, p. 40:
"Dove lavorai io, nella mia lunge vita, mai fui protetto da altri. Io mi sono protetto ed ho protetto..."

49. The Department of Justice's definition of "Organized Crime," as used by the Federal Bureau of Investigation:
"Any group having some manner of formalized structure and whose primary objective is to obtain money through illegal activities. Such groups maintain their position through the use of violence or threats of violence, corrupt public officials, graft or extortion and generally have a significant impact on the people in their locales or region or the country as a whole. One major crime group epitomizes this definition—La Cosa Nostra."

50. GENTILE, pp. 37-44.

51. *The Philadelphia Inquirer*, dated December 3, 1903.

52. GENTILE, p. 44:
"Ero nell'onorata societá da otto anni circa. Vi entrai a far parte a Filadelfia ma giá allora, a 21 anni di etá, il mio nome era noto a Boston e a Chicago."

53. Philadelphia Police Homicide Reports, Volumes 4 and 5, including homicides from August 26, 1914 to September 24, 1922.

54. HESS, p. 103.

55. Philadelphia Police Homicide Reports, Volume 3, dated November 21, 1909, June 21, 1913 and July 19, 1914.

56. WILLIAM J. FLYNN, *The Barrel Mystery*, (1919), pp. 206-214, 243-261.

57. PITKIN, p. 132.

58. GENTILE, p. 17:
"Negli Stati Uniti, come in Sicilia, la mafia cooperó quasi ininterrottamente con la polizia 'per mantenere l'ordine pubblico' e cioé nella liquidazione di banditi e gangsters 'non autorizzati' allo scopo di ottenere in cambio una certa 'zona di rispetto' per se stessa."

59. As referenced in Cressey and in JOSEPH ALBINI, *The American Mafia: Genesis of a Legend*, (New York: Appleton-Century-Crofts, 1971).

60. GENTILE, pp.44-45.

61. JOSEPH BONANNO, *A Man of Honor: An Autobiography*, (New York: Simon and Schuster, 1983), pp. 62-3.

62. The best source for early Italian-speaking settlers in Philadelphia is RICHARD N. JULIANI'S *Building Little Italy*, (University Park: Pennsylvania State University Press, 1997), as well as in Juliani's other works.

63. Philadelphia Police Homicide Reports.

64. GARY W. POTTER and PHILIP JENKINS, *The City and The Syndicate: Organized Crime in Philadelphia*, (Lexington: Ginn Press, 1985), pp. 33-35.

65. *Associated Press* article by HOPE YEN, dated September 8, 1999.

• • • • • • • •

Notes to Part II

● ●

1. Interview of Harry Riccobene in October, 1992, and subsequent interviews in 1993 to 1999.

2. Interviews taken of Sabella relatives in 1993 and 1994.

3. All English-speaking Philadelphia newspapers on June 1, 1927, through to the end of the month published the court testimony from *Commonwealth of Pennsylvania v. Avena, et al.* May Sessions, 1927. Clerk of the Quarter Sessions, Philadelphia, Pennsylvania.

4. FRANCHETTI and SONNINO, as referenced in Mack Smith, p. 474.

5. MACK SMITH, p. 496.

6. DUGGAN, p. 50; also, Mack Smith, p. 464.

7. *The London Times* of February 5, 1891.

8. G. AVELLONE and S. MORASCA, *Mafia*, (Rome: 1911), p. 118.

9. Interviews from Sabella relatives.

10. Department of Justice, Federal Bureau of Investigation File 92-8030/ 92-1377, Memorandum dated February 26, 1965, p. 9.

11. ARRIGO PETACCO, *Joe Petrosino*, (New York: 1974), pp. 135-149.

12. PITKIN, pp. 116-119.

13. MACK SMITH, p. 448.

14. MARTIN CLARK, *Modern Italy*, 1871-1982, (Singapore: The Print House, [Pte] Ltd., 1984), p. 88.

15. MACK SMITH, p. 464.

16. PITKIN, p. 21.

17. FBI File 92-445, dated December 2, 1964, p. 10; File 92-2790, dated February 17, 1967.

18. GENTILE, pp. 84 and 111.

19. Ibid., pp. 84 and 103.

20. BONANNO. pp. 84 and 120.

21. GENTILE, p. 13.

22. BONANNO, p. 270.

23. Philadelphia Police Homicide Reports.

24. PITKIN, p. 32.

25. RICHARD VARBERO, "The Politics of Ethnicity: Philadelphia's Italians in the 1920s" in Francisco Cordasco (Ed.), *Studies in Italian-American Social History*, (Totowa: Rowman & Littlefield, 1975), p. 176.

26. *The Philadelphia Evening Bulletin* of May 10, 1923.

27. *The Philadelphia Inquirer* and *The Public Ledger* of May 10, 1923.

28. Interviews of Sabella relatives. FBI Memorandum from SAC PH, re: File 92-554, (date unintelligible), 1955, p. 3.

29. Interviews of Salvatore Cucinotta, MD, taken in 1992 and 1993.

30. Refer to article in *The Philadelphia Evening Bulletin* of August 18, 1925 for other information on underworld activities.

31. *The Philadelphia Inquirer* of September 14, 1925.

32. The Pennsylvania Crime Commission Reports of 1970 and 1990, and Potter & Jenkins, pp. 33-36 have interesting versions of this event without reviewing the contemporary newspapers and court documents.

33. The men who would follow Sabella as boss of the Philadelphia Mafia/ La Cosa Nostra directly after he stepped down were present at this incident. The names and years of tenures as bosses are: John Avena (1931-1936), Joseph Bruno (1936-1946), Joseph Ida (1946-1959) and A. Domenico Pollina (1959).

34. All of the Philadelphia newspapers published accounts of these murders from the May 31, 1927 edition through to the end of June in 1927. Some details of the event were corroborated, then confirmed to produce the composite in the text.

35. Interviews of HARRY RICCOBENE from 1992 and 1993.

36. FRANCHETTI and SONNINO, as cited in Blok, p. 98.

37. Ibid.

38. PINO ARLACCHI, *Mafia Business: The Mafia Ethic & The Spirit of Capitalism*, (New York: Oxford University Press, 1988), p. 27.

39. GAMBETTA, pp. 75-99.

40. HESS, p. 68.

41. Ibid., p. 98.

42. *The Philadelphia Public Ledger,* May 31, 1927.

43. *The Philadelphia Inquirer,* June 15, 1927.

44. Philadelphia Police Homicide report of March 20, 1919, Volume 5.

45. *The Philadelphia Public Ledger*, June 15, 1927.

46. Ibid., and the May 31, 1927 edition.

47. *Commonwealth v. Avena, et al*. May Sessions, 1927, #1528, et seq.

48. Ibid.

49. FBI File 92-2931, dated May 31, 1966, pp. 11-12.

50. *Commonwealth v. Avena, et al.*

51. Confidential interviews.

52. Philadelphia Police Department's Index of Arrests. A recapitulation of the Lanzettis' lives is also found in FRANK BROOKHOUSER'S article, "The Brief, Lurid Lives of the Three Brothers in Death," *The Philadelphia Evening Bulletin,* dated March 9, 1969.

53. Gopsill's City Directories of Philadelphia, 1895 to 1900. The father's surname is often spelled, "Lanzetta."

54. *The Philadelphia Evening Bulletin*, February 5, 1935.

55. News accounts about the Lanzettis beating the rap were extremely frequent. From the late 1920s to the mid-1930s, there were many accounts, too many to note here.

56. *The Philadelphia Evening Bulletin*, June 25, 1933.

57. *The Philadelphia Evening Bulletin*, September 29, 1933.

58. *The Philadelphia Evening Bulletin*, September 24, 1924.

59. NELLI, pp. 169, 290 and n42 grossly exaggerated the Lanzettis' importance by basing their reputations solely on the *Bulletin* articles. Also see the *Bulletin's* August 24, 1925 edition for more information.

60. Brookhouser's 1969 article; *The Philadelphia Evening Bulletin*, August 24, 1925.

61. Philadelphia Police Homicide report, August 19, 1925, Volume 7.

62. *The Philadelphia Evening Bulletin*, August 20 to 25, 1925.

63. Philadelphia Police Homicide report, August 19, 1925, Volume 7.

64. *Bulletin*, August 25, 1925; *Inquirer*, September 14, 1925; *Bulletin*, September 16, 1925.

65. Philadelphia Police Homicide report, August 2, 1926, Volume 7.

66. NELLI, p. 149.

67. PITKIN, p. 221.

68. DAVID R. JOHNSON, *American Law Enforcement: A History*, (Arlington Heights: Forum Press, Inc., 1981), p. 145.

69. Refer to DAVID R. JOHNSON, *Policing the Urban Underworld: The Impact of Crime on the Development of the American Police, 1800 to 1887*, (Philadelphia: Temple University Press, 1979). Also, ALLEN F. DAVIS and MARK HALLER, (Eds.), *The Peoples of Philadelphia*, (Philadelphia: Temple University Press, 1973).

70. SAM BASS WARNER, JR., *The Private City: Philadelphia in Three Periods of its Growth*, (Philadelphia: University of Pennsylvania Press, 1968), pp. 184-5.

71. Refer to DAVIS & HALLER.

72. *Narcotic Education: Edited Report of the Proceedings of the First World Conference on Narcotic Education,* Philadelphia, Pennsylvania, July 5 to 9, 1926, (Washington, D.C.: H.S. Middlemiss Company, 1926). Also see *The Philadelphia Inquirer,* September 14, 1925.

73. JOHNSON, *American Law Enforcement*, p. 143.

74. The only remaining Philadelphia Police's Records of Arrests of Alcohol Violators date from 1929 to 1931 and hardly represent a

true source of evidence. Confidential interviews from former boot-leggers and others who manufactured alcohol in South Philadelphia confirmed the rarity of arrests in this section of the city, especially if one was associated with Mafia members. Note also in Potter & Jenkins, pp. 35-36 that they deny any existing Mafia in Philadelphia during Prohibition and that the "true boot-legging elite" was the "Jewish Mob," (p. 34).

75. NELLI, p. 169.

76. *The Philadelphia Evening Bulletin*, June 15, 1928.

77. *Inquirer* and *Public Ledger*, July 4, 1928; Philadelphia Police Homicide report, July 4, 1928, Volume 7.

78. GENTILE, p. 17.

79. Ibid., p. 106.

80. *Report Crimes Survey Committee*, Law Association of Philadelphia, (Philadelphia: 1926)

81. FBI File 92-2937, dated October 8, 1958, p. 6. Also refer to Potter & Jenkins, p. 34.

82. *Bulletin,* March 28, 1951.

83. PITKIN, p. 226. Also refer to Potter & Jenkins, p. x.

84. One of Sabella's soldiers confirmed this, but there are some other sources to deny the *capo dei capi* title: MONTE S. FINKLESTEIN, *Separatism, The Allies, and The Mafia,* (Bethlehem: Lehigh University Press, 1998), p. 197, n7. Tommaso Buscetta and Antonino Calderone also corroborate this. Gentile and Bonanno give no precedent for the title in Sicily.

85. GENTILE, p. 19.

86. ABADINSKY, p. 51.

87. STEPHEN FOX, *Blood & Power: Organized Crime in Twentieth Century America,* (New York: William Morrow & Company, Inc., 1989), p. 67.

88. GENTILE, p. 6.

89. BONANNO, p. 84.

90. Ibid., pp. 100-102.

91. GENTILE, p. 104.

92. Ibid.

93. Interviews from Harry Riccobene; Gentile, p. 102:
"Dal 5 gennaio 1927...al settembre 30, 1930... erano trascorsi quasi quattro anni: Molto sangue era stato sparso a molte cose erano cambiate."

94. Interviews from Harry Riccobene in 1992 and 1993.

95. Philadelphia Police Department of Records, arrests of April, 1929.

96. Interviews from Harry Riccobene in 1992 and 1993.

97. Departments of Deeds and Real Estate, Montgomery County Courthouse, Norristown, Pennsylvania.

98. BONANNO, pp. 86-88.

99. Refer to this theory in explanation: FRANCIS A.J. IANNI, *Ethnic Succession in Organized Crime.* (Washington, D.C.: Government Printing Office, 1972), and in Ianni, *Black Mafia: Ethnic Succession in Organized Crime,* (New York: Simon & Schuster, 1974). Abadinsky's comments about these works are on pp. 54-55 in *Organized Crime.*

100. ALAN BLOCK, "Lepke, Kid Twist & The Combination: Organized Crime in New York City, 1930-1944," University of California at Los Angeles, California, Ph.D. dissertation, 1975, p. 228.

101. BONANNO, p. 70.

102. GENTILE, p. 101.

103. Ibid., p. 106.

104. Ibid., p. 104.

105. Interviews from Harry Riccobene in 1992 and 1993.

106. HESS, p. 93; also, Gentile, p. 65.

107. PINO ARLACCHI, *Men of Dishonor: Inside The Sicilian Mafia—An Account of Antonino Calderone,* (New York: Morrow & Company, 1993), pp. 33-35.

108. The FBI indices have the names of many individuals who could have been victims of the Castellammarese Wars, if using Gentile's time frame of January 5, 1927 to September 30, 1930. This would not, however, count Masseria (died, April 16, 1931) or Maranzano (died September 10, 1931), but would suggest a number comparable to the approximate "forty" who supposedly died. Abadinsky, p. 460, cited Alan Block's comments about the casualties, indicating that neither Abadinsky nor Block did not review the federal law

enforcement's records. Bonanno, pp. 18 to 143 documents several deaths, more in line to the FBI's estimate.

109. Actually, there are no reports of elderly Mafiosi among the dead. Refer to Bonanno, pp. 18 to 143 for his first-hand account on who was killed among the older members of the Organization. The reader is advised that the term, "greaser" applied to the Sicilian-born — if this was a "Greaser War," then Bonanno, Gambino and other young Mafiosi would have been killed at that time.

110. GENTILE, p. 106.

111. BONANNO, pp. 100-102.

112. GENTILE, p. 106.

113. *The New York Times*, April 18, 1931 and September 11, 1931.

114. *The New York Times*, April 16, 1931.

115. GENTILE, p. 112; Bonanno, pp. 138-140, 149-52, 162-3.

116. Ibid.

117. Interviews from Harry Riccobene in 1992 and 1993; Bonanno, pp. 136-43; Gentile, pp. 116-18.

118. FBI File 92-1489 (Philadelphia Office to SAC in Buffalo) File 92-594, dated June 23, 1965, p. 1-3, 7.

119. SAC in Newark, New Jersey's File 92-1986 to Philadelphia Office File 92-1377, dated December 2, 1964, pp. 1-2; SAC PH 92-1489 to SAC Buffalo 92-594, dated June 23, 1965, pp. 1-3; SAC Philadelphia File 92-444 to FBI Director 92-2717, dated January 21, 1965, p. 1. Bonanno, pp. 41 and 63 also corroborate the information in these reports.

120. Linden Police Department (Union County, New Jersey), Arrest #235, August 19, 1931; FBI SAC Newark to SAC Philadelphia File 92-1377, dated October 20, 1964, p. 1, and Memorandum dated December 2, 1964, p. 1.

121. GENTILE, p. 45.

122. *The New York Times*, September 11, 1931; Gentile, pp. 111-119 adds more to Capone's interest in Maranzano's death.

123. Interview from Salvatore J. Avena, Esquire in 1999.

124. FBI Memorandum to SAC in Philadelphia Office, re: File 92-1377, dated December 3, 1964, p. 3. Also, *Commonwealth v. Avena, et al.*

125. Ibid.

126. Pennsylvania Crime Commission Report of 1990, p. 153.

127. Philadelphia Police Homicide Report, October 27, 1928, Volume 8.

128. *Public Ledger*, June 15, 1927.

129. *Commonwealth v. Quaranta*, January Term, 1928, #322. Clerk of the Quarter Sessions of Philadelphia County. Also, FBI Memorandum dated December 1, 1964 from SAC, re: File 92-1027, pp. 3-4. Also refer to the Philadelphia newspaper accounts, such as in *The Inquirer* and *Daily News*. *The New York Times* also printed an account on September 9, 1935.

130. Interviews from Sabella relatives. Also, FBI Washington, D.C. File 92-8030 to Philadelphia Office File 92-1377, dated November 10, 1964, pp. 1-2. And, Montgomery County arrest records of March 29, 1935.

131. Ibid.

132. GENTILE, p. 25: "Ammazzare tutti gli sciaccatani."

133. FBI SAC Philadelphia File 92-1489 to SAC in Buffalo File 92-594, dated June 23, 1965, pp. 9-10.

134. Philadelphia Police Records of Arrests in February of 1940. FBI Philadelphia Office File 92-1377/ BU File 92-8030 (no date), p. 7 also has Sabella's occupation: "storekeeper, self-employed in a cigar store at *********, Philadelphia, Pennsylvania. He also operated a meat market in *********** during the years 1940 to 1946. No employment indicated for Salvatore Sabella since 1946." (Asterisks added for confidentiality.) Memorandum dated December 3, 1964, p. 1 and Memo to Buffalo, dated June 23, 1965, pp. 9-10.

135. Department of Justice, Immigration and Naturalization Service File on Salvatore Sabella. Also, FBI File PH 92-1377, dated February 9, 1965, p. 24.

136. There are a number of books published as popular titles that contain this information. They are not scholarly books, nor are they construed to be. Among them are: J. ROBERT NASH, *Encyclopedia of World Crime,* (Wilmette: CrimeBooks, Inc., 1989)

137. *Commonwealth v. Salvatore Sabella,* November Term, 1943, #443-444. Philadelphia County, Pennsylvania.

138. FBI Philadelphia Office File 92-1377, dated February 9, 1965, p. 11.

139. Philadelphia Police Records of Arrests, September, 1943. Also, FBI Philadelphia Office File 92-1377, dated February 9, 1965, p. 16.

140. FBI Washington, D.C. Office File 92-8030 to Philadelphia Office, dated September 28, 1964, pp. 1-3.

141. FBI SAC Philadelphia Office File 92-444 to FBI Director's File 92-2717, dated January 21, 1965, p. 1; FBI SAC Philadelphia Office File 92-1489 to SAC in Buffalo Office, re: File 92-594, dated June 23, 1965, pp. 1-3.

142. FBI Washington, D.C. File 92-8030 to Philadelphia Office File 92-1377, dated August 30, 1946, citing July 18, 1946 letter from Chicago FBI Office.

143. FBI Washington, D.C. File 92-8030 to SAC in Philadelphia, re: File: 92-1377, dated September 28, 1964, pp. 1-3; INS File #A5579668, December 24, 1940.

144. FBI Philadelphia Office Memorandum, re: File 92-1377, dated February 9, 1965, p. 18.

145. *Bulletin*, August 24, 1950.

146. Ibid.

147. *Bulletin*, March 21, 1951.

148. After the two investigations in the early 1950s failed to conclude the Mafia/La Cosa Nostra's existence in Philadelphia, Police Commissioner Thomas J. Gibbons, "admitted there is a segment of the Mafia—organized crime syndicate—in Philadelphia." Source: *Bulletin*, February 17, 1958.

149. *Inquirer*, October 24, 1951.

150. Interviews with Sabella friends and relatives in 1993 and 1994.

151. FBI Philadelphia Office File 92-1377, re: 62-2122-4, p. 14, citing letter from Chicago FBI Office to Director, dated July 18, 1946.

152. Interviews from Sabella family members.

153. FBI Philadelphia Office File 92-1377, "Office Request," dated September 28, 1964, p. 1, including period from October 30, 1952 to April 30, 1952.

154. FBI Philadelphia Office File 92-1377, dated February 9, 1965, p. 10 and Washington, D.C. File 92-8030, dated February 9, 1965, pp. 3-4. Some Philadelphia newspapers also published reports on the death of Joseph Pane, also known as, "Pepe Longo." See *Inquirer* and *Bulletin* stories from April 6-7, 1950 for more information. Another source: Philadelphia Police Homicide report, April 5, 1950: "unsolved."

155. FBI Philadelphia Office File 92-1377, dated February 9, 1965, pp. 17-18.

156. Hess, *Mafia and Mafiosi*, p. 53.

157. Danilo Dolci, *Spreco: Documenti e inchieste su alcuni aspetti nella Sicilia occidentale,* (Turin: 1960), pp. 68-9.

158. Indro Montanelli, *Pantheon Minore,* (Milan: 1958), p. 282.

159. Commonwealth of Pennsylvania, Department of Vital Statistics. Also, FBI Philadelphia Office File 92-1489, "Memorandum" to SAC in Buffalo Office, File 92-594, dated June 23, 1965, p. 8; FBI "Memorandum" to SAC in Philadelphia, File 92-1377, dated December 11, 1964, p. 1.

• • • • • • • • •

Acknowledgements

● ●

An historian is only as good as his/her sources. Accordingly, the subject matter of this work was edified by extraordinary individuals whose sincerity was well appreciated. I thank the Sabella family, Santo Agati, Esq., Salvatore J. Avena, Esq., Joseph DiMino, DO, Anne Fabbri, Harry Riccobene, John Sardisco, MD, my relatives and my Sicilian American friends for their moments of honesty about this sensitive issue of our foreign culture and its remnants. I also acknowledge those who have passed on during the course of this work for what courage their disclosures brought for the sake of an accurate historical record.

Otherwise noted references do not name particular individuals who recognized my need for information and to review primary sources. Among them are retired Philadelphia Police Inspector of the Homicide Unit, Jerrold Kane who eased my way in research since 1992 and who was followed in kind by Homicide Captains Thomas Quinn and Stephen Glenn. Eight years is a long time to collect, to disseminate and to try not to become discouraged with the paucity of information available but these Finest of

Philadelphia's law enforcement, along with Lieutenant Harry Giordano of the Records and Identification Unit are owed my gratitude for more than their patience. They provided records which future scholars will find infinitely useful. I will also never forget former assistant chief of the United States Attorney's Office's Organized Crime Strike Force, Albert C. Wicks for years of friendship and inspiration, and for providing me with information to further my research on the local La Cosa Nostra.

Spending several years on this book was not without qualms on how best to execute such an elusive subject. I am therefore grateful to many for their special assistance: my finished work owes much to the critical eye of Mr. Joseph Casino, instructor of History at St. Joseph's University and Villanova University; Mr. Frank Szerbin of Jefferies & Manz composed, designed and detailed this book for visual ease; Richard Boardman from the Free Library of Philadelphia's Map Collection again selected the most appropriate maps for use; John F. Seidler guided the production of this book gracefully to completion; and,

Lastly, *ma bedda matri* gets some credit because she is my link to my foreign culture's traditions and customs, and to my Honored ancestors in Sicily .

• • • • • • • • •

Special thanks to following
• •

United States Department of Justice
U.S. Attorney's Office, Organized Crime Strike Force
Federal Bureau of Investigation,
Washington, D.C. and Philadelphia Offices
Immigration & Naturalization Service

Commonwealth of Pennsylvania Department of Corrections
State Correctional Institute at Dallas

Courthouses of
Camden County, New Jersey, and
Montgomery County, Pennsylvania

Clerk of the Quarter Sessions for Philadelphia County,
Pennsylvania

The Philadelphia Police

Norristown Police

Bristol Borough Police and Chief Frank Peranteau

Historical Society of Montgomery County, Pennsylvania

Free Library of Philadelphia

College of Physicians, Philadelphia

Jenkins Law Library, Philadelphia

Pennsylvania State University, University Park, Pennsylvania

Temple University Urban Archives, Philadelphia

Villanova University, Villanova, Pennsylvania

St. Mary Magdalen de Pazzi Roman Catholic Church, Philadelphia

• • • • • • • • •

Index